M000305205

Letters to Her

Becoming a Woman of Purity, Purpose, and Proverbs 31 Virtue

Letters to Her

BECOMING A WOMAN OF PURITY, PURPOSE, AND PROVERBS 31 VIRTUE

JENNIFER IMEDIEGWU

Carpenter's Son Publishing

Letters to Her: Becoming a Woman of Purity, Purpose, and Proverbs 31 Virtue

©2018 by Jennifer Imediegwu

All rights reserved. No part of this book may be reproduced or transmitted in any form or by any means, electronic or mechanical, including photocopying, recording or by any information storage and retrieval system, without permission in writing from the copyright owner.

Published by Carpenter's Son Publishing, Franklin, Tennessee.

Published in association with Larry Carpenter of Christian Book Services, LLC. www.christianbookservices.com

Scripture taken from THE HOLY BIBLE, NEW INTERNATIONAL VERSION®, NIV® Copyright © 1973, 1978, 1984, 2011 by Biblica, Inc.™ Used by permission. All rights reserved worldwide.

Scripture is used from the New King James Version, © 1982 by Thomas Nelson, Inc. All rights reserved. Used by permission.

Scripture quotations taken from the Amplified® Bible, Copyright © 1954, 1958, 1962, 1964, 1965, 1987 by The Lockman Foundation Used by permission. (www.Lockman.org)

The Holy Bible, Berean Study Bible, BSB, Copyright ©2016, 2018 by Bible Hub. Used by Permission. All Rights Reserved Worldwide.

Scripture taken from the Holy Bible, NEW INTERNATIONAL READER'S VERSION®.Copyright © 1996, 1998 Biblica. All rights reserved throughout the world. Used by permission of Biblica.

Edited by Adept Content Solutions

Cover and Interior Layout Design by Suzanne Lawing

Printed in the United States of America

978-1-946889-69-0

Dedication

*To all the women longing for an
exceptional life in God's will.*

ACKNOWLEDGMENTS

To my Lord and Savior Jesus Christ. Thank you for the very air I breathe and this moment in time to share with your daughters the word you put in my heart. I am humbled by your redeeming love and grace, and I am nothing without you. I pray that this book will bless your daughters beyond what I can imagine, and may your Name alone be glorified.

To my sweet parents, Mr. Crawford and Mrs. June Webb. Thank you for your sacrifice, endless love, ongoing support, faith in God, and for always believing in me. You went to great lengths to provide me a foundation of Christian faith, family values, and education that will carry me through the rest of my life, and for that I am forever grateful to you. Thank you for exemplifying great character and integrity and for having hearts of gold. Your generous spirit has touched every person you have encountered. I love you.

To my amazing husband, Chino Imediegwu. You are an honorable man, and it is an honor to be your wife and the mother of your children. Thank you for your vision for our lives and the leadership of our home. Thank you for supporting my dreams and believing in me from the first day we met. Thank you for the overflowing love you have for me and our sweet boys. I'm enjoying doing life with you. Forever I am my Beloved's and my Beloved is mine.

To my wonderful mum- and dad-in-law, Dr. Obioha and Mrs. Ibironke Imediegwu. Thank you for your amazing love for God and faithfulness to His Word. You laid a biblical foundation in your four children, and I am blessed to be your daughter-in-law, married to your first-born child. Thank you for being prayer warriors. You have won many battles on your knees and changed your family tree. I am forever grateful for your counsel, love, and stellar example of a godly marriage. My regards and love to you both.

To my handsome, smart, sweet, amazing three sons: Joshua, Jordan, and Jonathan. You triple my joy in life. When I look at the three of you, I see the very best of your father and me, so wonderfully woven together. I am humbled and grateful to God for smiling on us and blessing us with you boys. I have no doubt you will go far in life and be the best at whatever you set your hands to do. Remember, you are not talented for your own gain, but called to do great things for God's glory.

To Bishop Michael E. Hill and First Lady Pearl Hill of Kingdom International Church of God in Christ. Thank you for being my spiritual parents. Bishop Hill, thank you for your sound biblical teaching. God transformed my life under your leadership, and I am forever grateful to your ministry. Momma Hill, thank you for being my modern-day Naomi and guiding me to my Boaz! You are such a Proverbs 31 woman, and I am forever grateful for the time we walked closely together. We laughed together, cried together, ate together, and shopped together! Just being girls together and absorbing your essence, grace, and elegance was a gift from God. Thank you.

To my big sister, Tonya Ford, and your three beautiful princesses: Arianna, Alania, and Amia Ford. Thank you, Sister, for your support, encouragement, and constant presence in my life. You have always showered me with love, and I am grateful for you, and I love you dearly. Girls, keep shining for Jesus and strive to do your best at every level in life. All three of you have amazing potential. Let the greatness come forth. I love you.

To Simone McKinney, Morgan Moss, the late Eboni Johnson, Tiffany Johnson, and Shevon Coles. God put you ladies in my life at the right time and right season, thank you for your beautiful honest friendship.

To friends, family, and colleagues all too many to name here by name, thank you. Thank you for your love, kindness, support, and all the many things you have done to bless my journey.

Contents

Preface 15

Introduction 17

Letter #1: My Heart's Cry 25

Letter #2: Dying on the Threshold 33

Letter #3: To Eden I Go 57

Letter #4: Daughters of Destiny 69

Letter #5: At Her Feet I Supped 87

Letter #6: Let's Be Girls Together 99

Letter #7: Readied for My King 113

Letter #8: Refreshed for a
          New Beginning 135

Notes 145

PREFACE

Why is it so difficult to be a woman of purity, purpose, and Proverbs 31 virtue?

The resistance every woman faces, both internally and externally, is the cause of this difficulty. Paul describes the struggle in Romans: "For I have the desire to do what is good, but I cannot carry it out. For I do not do the good I want to do, but the evil I do not want to do—this I keep on doing."[1] This is the battle every woman faces, and she must decide who she will be, what will define her, and, ultimately, whom she will serve.

Every Christian woman has this battle between her flesh and her spirit. It is the struggle of her own desires versus what God requires. It is the resistance of independence to the spirit of submission. It is the flesh-defying quest of finding "me" when we exist in a lost and dying world. It is finding the depth of her soul, purity of her heart, and godliness in her lifestyle when society promotes materialism, sexiness, and temporary bliss. It is the reverberating yet life-defining question of what is my purpose and destiny, where is my place in God, and ultimately how do these things all align within this realm called marriage? This battle takes place behind the closed doors of her mind, her heart, and even her home. This is the journey we will take in *Letters to Her.*

INTRODUCTION

Throughout my life I have seen a lot of relational and financial strife around me, both in my family and community. Growing up, I saw divorce, out of wedlock births, drug addiction, and brokenness of varying degrees. Consequently, I became intrigued with understanding why these things were so pervasive. Certainly poor decisions come to mind at the micro level and broader social injustices and political strife at the macro level, but there had to be something deeper. I wanted to ultimately understand, at a much deeper level, what was different about those who push through hard circumstances and rise above their brokenness and enjoy wholeness and a full robust life, compared to those who acquiesce to the pressures, never fulfilling their potential. Very early on in life I realized that success in *all* areas of my life was directly tied to the creator of this universe. I realized to go higher, meant to go deeper in Him, and that required me to surrender my life to Jesus, let him be Lord over every area, and keep pressing by faith daily whether it is sunny or not, popular or not, or easy or not. It meant taking hold of something bigger than me and never letting go.

Over the last decade, I have had an extraordinary journey of meeting women of all ages, various ethnic groups, and economic backgrounds. Some encounters led to deeper and more meaningful relationships while others were simply acquaintances, colleagues, neighbors, or fellow church members. These many unplanned encounters were simply the result of life's journey: being on a university campus, involved in the community, planted in a church, or going to work day in and day out. We are all familiar with that pace, the humdrum of life and the routines to keep it going, but little did I know something deeper was going on. God was connecting me to certain people who would thrust me into my destiny, as well as connect me to others to serve as a source of encouragement and wisdom to help them grow and reach their God-sized destiny too. Simultaneously, this last decade has brought forth the development and revelation of the relationships we do not get to choose, which is family. I have spent time reflecting on my various family relationships, understanding, and appreciating the gifts and lessons my family has given me both directly and indirectly.

However, when I reflect over the last ten years, what I recognize most is the process of building my life's foundation. This is the testimony I seek to share in the next eight heartfelt letters to my Sisters as tangible tools to help you succeed at answering life's most difficult questions. It was the revelation of God's Word that comforted me, but most importantly transformed me. Regardless of the backdrop of the story of your life or how extreme you think your brokenness or failures are, it is my prayer that the insights and truths of this book come bursting forth like the dawn of the fresh morning sun that you may see hope, healing, and your destiny before you.

This book is a testament to the decade-long journey of finding my first love, Jesus Christ, and coming into my complete sense of womanhood of who I am and called to be. Secondly, it is about establishing godly relationships with friends and mentors for accountability and encouragement in the journey ahead. Lastly, this book reflects on the process of becoming a wife for the husband God created me for, and being sold out for the vision He put in us for His glory and kingdom impact. These tools and revelations transformed my life, and I want to put them into your hands so that you, too, can build a God-sized destiny.

I initially put forward the question, "What is the difference between those who rise above their brokenness and those who shrink back and never achieve their full potential?" I will explore the answer to this in more detail, but we must first recognize that, even as Christians, we must make conscientious decisions and put forth intentional effort to improve our circumstances. Salvation does not instantly eradicate the negative plight we face as individuals. However, Christ in us gives us the power to walk in victory. This walk begins after you have accepted Jesus Christ. At that point you have eternal life, but after you are done rejoicing about the beauty of your afterlife, you yet have to deal with the things of this life. What does this life contain? Well, it contains your past, present, future, hopes, fears, shortcomings, trials, and tribulations.

I know you were hoping that God would zap all of those things away and give you a cloud nine euphoric bubble to float through life in before going on to heaven; however, it does not work that way, and the book of Job says that man is born of a few days and those few days are filled with trouble.[2] The blessing is that we do not have to be defeated in our troubles and live in misery, but we can have peace and joy in the midst of the challenging circumstances. Christ came that we would have life and have it more abundantly, and until He returns, His Holy Spirit will be a comforter, a teacher of all things, and a guide into all truth.[3] He said He would never leave us nor forsake us and not only is He with us, but His Holy Spirit in us gives us power to tread upon the serpent's head, rebuke demons and devils, and pull down strongholds.[4]

Many sociologists would say that people are a product of their environment. It is commonly believed that our lives are the result of our environments, upbringing, experiences, and genetic predispositions. For example, if you were abused, you will continue to be abused or become an abuser. If you were born into poverty, and all you have known and experienced is poverty, then you will die in poverty. This is the self-perpetuation of naturally occurring cycles; once it is set in motion, things typically tend to keep moving in the same direction. But I have news for you: that does not have to be the life of a Christian. These things would be so, except there is intervention. Education can remedy the woes of poverty, but what can remedy the pains and wounds of your soul? Sister, Jesus Christ saves, sanctifies, and sets free. Without divine intervention, your life will remain stagnant; you will repeat unhealthy decisions, and your spirit will languish in despair and defeat.

I want this book to not be the proverbial self-help book but to be the starting point of discovering you, your destiny, and your Lord. I want this book to elevate your thinking and be so thought provoking that it spurs action in your life. I want it to be an eye-opening journey for the Christian new bride or young maiden looking to marry, to discover and understand what it truly means to become a prudent wife. Or, for the married woman who has toiled away at the commitment of marriage and needs a cool refreshing for the journey ahead. Ready your hearts for a journey that is least traveled but most rewarding, because a godly woman is a queen among women. She is a rare jewel, and her price is far above rubies.[5] She is timeless, invaluable, and absolutely stunning. She is hidden in God—someone only a man after God's own heart can find.

I learned that courage was not the absence of fear, but the triumph over it. The brave man is not he who does not feel afraid, but he who conquers that fear.

NELSON MANDELA

Letter #1:

MY HEART'S CRY

My Beloved Sister,

You have found yourself reading this book beyond the introduction, so I take it that you have personally asked yourself the questions that this book will address. Perhaps you have asked yourself, in one way or another, one of the three following questions:

1) Why do I continue to make unhealthy decisions?

2) I'm a Christian woman, wanting to live for God, but how do I really get a foothold on my destiny?

3) How can I become a godly wife?

Whether you have asked yourself one or all these questions, I promise this book will be a great investment in your spiritual walk as you mature as a Christian and a wife. I guarantee there will be at least a dozen insightful nuggets you can take away that will change your life radically. We are all in this common place, reading this book right now, because there is a voice within all of us that says, "I want to be the woman God is calling me to be and I want to start today." You see, this book is not for the dreamers who keep on dreaming and never wake up.

This is for the divas in Christ who are ready to take their stilettos to a higher place. You are no longer just interested in the new handbags or styles and colors for each season. You realize that your value is more than skin deep and there are areas in your life Mary Kay, MAC, or CoverGirl can't cover up. I am talking about restoration and rejuvenation like you have never seen before, and it is better than a sugar scrub and vitamin exfoliating spa treatment with massage. Really, it is! Trust me in this.

> THIS IS FOR THE DIVAS IN CHRIST WHO ARE READY TO TAKE THEIR STILETTOS TO A HIGHER PLACE.

I am talking about having the kind of depth and intimacy with God that is so invigorating it will take your breath away and have your soul panting for more. It is a place in God that people seldom reach for because it takes time, discipline, sacrifice, and consistency—all of which are contrary to twenty-first-century living but are necessary for you to really become the woman God is calling you to be and will equip you to fulfill your destiny.

We are going to be addressing some tough issues— things rather ignored than confronted. This may require you to look into your past for answers, look eye to eye with your mother, or even look into the mirror at yourself. We may cry as we read, think, reflect, and act, but if you take what is said in this book seriously and apply it, you will have set in motion a new you and most importantly the will of God. Even if you mess up, after soaking up every bit of wisdom bursting forth in the upcoming pages, get back up and apply it. If things get hard and it seems more

APPLY THESE TRUTHS CONTINUALLY AND YOU WILL FOREVER WALK IN VICTORY.

comfortable and convenient to shrink back, stand firm and apply it. Apply these truths continually and you will forever walk in victory.

I am not writing this to preach to you. You all are my Sisters and I want God's best for you. Many of us may not cross paths with each other, but the connecting fiber we all share is that we are women and Christ is our Lord. This comes with a similar journey we all must tread which provides us the treasures we can share with each other and cause each other to grow and live a life full of purpose and God's glory.

I want this to be a journey of us walking, talking, laughing, and learning together. In fact, I encourage you to read this with a select group of friends. You'll be amazed at how discussion is ignited, and going the journey together will create an accountability circle where everyone has someone to pray with and seek encouragement from when the going gets tough. I'm writing to you, my Sisters, with passion and love like Paul wrote to the church thousands of years ago. No, this is not a new age Bible I have penned. Please scrap that thought! It is a work that I pray will inspire you on your journey with God and cause a thirst and hunger for Him like never before.

You see, this world has become so fast paced, and everyone is fighting to get ahead while chasing the American Dream. People work all day, and yet at night their minds are up walking the floor lunging into the next day even before daybreak. For so many people, in

LET US BECOME THE GENERATION THAT GOD WILL POUR OUT HIS SPIRIT UPON COLLECTIVELY.

all their pursuits they yet come up short, realizing later in life that there was more to riches and fame or the chasing of it all, which they never attained. I write to you because it is my heart's cry that you not take such a meaningless and disappointing path. Let us become the generation that will seek Him. Let us become the generation that God will pour out His Spirit upon collectively. Let us be the women He calls daughters, and along with His sons we will establish His kingdom on earth.

Are you ready to get about the King's business? Are you ready to trade the ashes of your dreams for the beauty of His will?[6]

If so, enter in . . .

From a submitted heart to yours,
Jennifer

Questions TO PONDER AND DISCUSS

1. When you quiet yourself, what are the concerns that pull at your heart?

2. What sort of messaging are you bombarded with via the television, internet, and social media?

3. How would you describe your relationship with God? What would you change, if anything?

A *Prayer* TO PRAY

Dear Lord, as I embark on this journey of purity, purpose, and Proverbs 31 virtue, I ask that you cleanse me, give me clarity about your will for my life, and develop me into a virtuous woman. Help me to be who you are calling me to be, and to not be defined by the world's definitions and symbols of beauty, power, and independence. Do a marvelous work in me, that you alone may be glorified. Open my eyes and ears to the revelation of your Word and help me to listen and obey. Help me to not shrink back in fear, but to stand bold on your Word. Lord, I know that you have not given me a spirit of fear, but of power, love, and a sound mind, and I receive it today. Finally, Lord, I ask that you connect me with other women I can take this journey with, who have a heart to honor you. May there be trust, accountability, and healing.

In Jesus' Name I pray. Amen.

I cannot think of any need in childhood as strong as the need for a father's protection.

SIGMUND FREUD

Letter #2:

DYING ON THE THRESHOLD

My Beloved Sister,

"*When we were kids we used to have to walk three miles to school, sometimes barefoot, and when we got home in the evening, mother had supper ready. After we ate, we did the homework Ms. Janey sent home in our satchels. We didn't have televisions and tablets and such. If you were really lucky, you had a good radio to listen to shows on. For fun, we used to go to the five-cent show, play hand games, and when we were old enough hanging out at the ice-cream parlor and dancing to the jukebox was the cool thing to do.*"

Aren't these the stories, or some variation of it, handed down from generation to generation with much laughter of how the times have changed? I remember vivid stories my parents shared about old technology and the good ole' days when the entire neighborhood knew everyone and their children. Neighbors could even lay a strap to one or two of them if they got beside themselves! These are the stories that go down in history, often passed around at the dinner table, and sometimes captured in new films reflecting old times. However, I am curious about who is writing on the scroll of their children's hearts the truths of life that will make him or her responsible, disciplined, and upright? Who is taking their past mistakes and turning them into powerful messages that will pave the way to victory for their children, our future? When the family institution is the cornerstone of our society, who is hearing the voice of our young daughters nervously crying out?

Can I ask you a question, Mother? What was your real story, Mother? We know the financial struggle and the political struggles. But what was your heart's struggle as a young woman? What were your thoughts when you gazed into the endless sky? Who did you yearn for as your eyes searched the vast sea? Who, Mother, who? Mother, I'm feeling like a woman now, and I'd like to be with a man. Who was your "first" mother? What does "it" feel like? He tells me it feels good and there's no feeling like it. Is that true? I think I'm ready. He seems to be a really nice guy. He said I'm the only girl he wants. Mother? Mother, do you hear me?

SILENCE.

SILENCE.

SILENCE.

Mother won't talk to me. Or perhaps she just doesn't know. I guess I can do this thing on my own.

This is the reality so many of us grew up in. We heard the cute little stories of how life was on the farm, in the years of the Great Depression, in the village, or wherever life began for our ancestors. We have seen how technology has progressed and we understand why Grandpa does not text message or why Mom still is holding on to her record player even though we are in the digital age. Those are great stories to recount, but are we really talking about real life issues? Did your mother talk about the hardcore truths concerning sex, drugs, and every other destructive vice? More than likely she did not, or perhaps she did, but the discussion lacked detail and frequency. This is certainly no indictment against her, because chances are she was born into the generation that thought sex was a taboo. It was an uncomfortable subject for her to bring up, because her mother may not have provided such teaching and encouraged such open discussion either.

WE ARE LIVING IN A TIME WHERE THE STORY OF THE BIRDS AND THE BEES IS INSUFFICIENT.

We are living in a time where the story of the birds and the bees is insufficient. Sex has remained a taboo conversationally amongst older generations, but progressively has become socially exploited in America. Sex is everywhere, sex sells, and it is preying on families' homes, including Christians. The hard truth is that just because parents are not opening their mouths to discuss it, does not mean that their daughters are not opening their legs to it. I apologize for how vulgar this sounds, but sometimes we need to be jolted out of our comfort zones because that is where the enemy has lulled us to sleep.

Statistics reveal this is a serious issue and the rates of sexually transmitted diseases (STDs) are climbing according to the Centers for Disease Control and

Prevention Annual Report (CDC). In particular, between 2014 and 2015, cases of primary and secondary syphilis grew 19 percent, gonorrhea grew 12.8 percent, and chlamydia grew 5.9 percent. According to the website for the Centers for Disease Control and Prevention among U.S. High School students surveyed in 2015:[7]

- 41 percent had ever had sexual intercourse.

- 30 percent had sexual intercourse during the previous 3 months, and, of these:
    o 43 percent did not use a condom the last time they had sex;
    o 14 percent did not use any method to prevent pregnancy; and
    o 21 percent had drunk alcohol or used drugs before last sexual intercourse.

- Only 10 percent of sexually experienced students have ever been tested for human immunodeficiency virus (HIV).

- Young people (aged 13–24) accounted for an estimated 22 percent of all new HIV diagnoses in the United States in 2014.

- Among young people (aged 13–24) diagnosed with HIV in 2014, 80 percent were gay and bisexual males.

- Half of the nearly 20 million new STDs reported each year were among young people, between the ages of 15 to 24.

- Nearly 250,000 babies were born to teen girls aged 15–19 years in 2014.

Premarital sex has become a norm in our country,

and the median number of sexual partners for men and women are seven and four respectively.[8] The basic point I am making is that just because the conversation is not taking place, does not mean that the hormones are not raging, the pressures are not present, and poor decisions are not made.

LOW SELF-ESTEEM, MISTAKING LUST FOR LOVE, AND WANTING TO FEEL LIKE AN ADULT ARE COMMON LIES THAT ENSNARE.

What I find to be most upsetting about this set of circumstances is that many times, these girls are so oblivious to the value of what they are giving away. Low self-esteem, mistaking lust for love, and wanting to feel like an adult are common lies that ensnare, and many do not realize the costs of these decisions.

So, what *really* happens to a young girl when she's exposed to a man before being exposed to righteousness? Well, let's explore the story of a young girl from Bethlehem whose pain-filled testimony is hidden in the Old Testament and seldom recounted. It is tucked away in the book of Judges, and in the New International Version (NIV) Bible, the story is entitled "A Levite and his Concubine."

A LOST DAUGHTER

Judges chapter 19 reveals to us the biblical version of our daughters who are lost and have been warped by ill-intentioned men. It is the story of a young girl from Bethlehem who grew up in a time when lawlessness reigned. Verse one says: "In those days Israel had no king." A standard of righteousness and sense of governing authority was absent, and each man did as he saw fit. There was a Levite living in a remote area who came to Bethlehem and took this young girl as his concubine. I must pause here and reiterate she was taken not to be his wife but to be a concubine. A concubine is a woman who lives with a man but who is not a wife. She is considered a slave girl for sexual service in which the male is the dominant partner and she is attached to him solely for the purpose of reproduction. She was not taken as a wife to be loved and cared for; instead, she was taken to be used. She was deemed no more valuable than a whore.

In the cultural setting of that time, women were not highly esteemed and often thought of as property. Let us also think of this in a modern-day perspective when it says, "He took a concubine from Bethlehem." This was somebody's daughter, a precious child. Where were her parents to say, "No, she is worth more than that. Her price is far above rubies, which you cannot afford if you are simply looking for a concubine"? Of course, there is no record of such a thing; perhaps her family was poor and needed the money she could be traded for. This is mere speculation, but what we do know is that she ends up with him in the remote place of Ephraim.

The story progresses in Judges 19:18–30. The concubine becomes unfaithful to the Levite, leaves him, and returns to her father's home. After four months, the Levite came for her to persuade her to return. She took him into her father's house, and when her father saw him, he gladly welcomed him. Her father constantly prevailed upon him to stay, so he remained there several days eating and drinking. After feasting several days, the man was determined to leave. He took his two saddled donkeys and his concubine and headed in the direction of Jebus (Jerusalem). When it became too dark for travel, they began looking for lodging. Finally, an old man offered to allow them to stay with him. While they were eating and drinking, some wicked men began pounding on the door and shouting to the old man, "Bring out the man who is staying with you, so we can have sex with him."

The old man stepped outside to talk to them. "No, my brothers, don't do such an evil thing. For this man is a guest in my house, and such a thing would be shameful. Here, take my virgin daughter and this man's concubine. I will bring them out to you, and you can use them and do whatever you wish. But don't do such a shameful thing to this man." The Levite took hold of his concubine and pushed her out the door, and the men of the town abused her all night, taking turns raping her until morning. Finally, at dawn, they let her go.

So, how does this story end? At daybreak, the woman returned to the house where the Levite was staying. She collapsed at the door of the house and lay there until it was light. When the Levite opened the door to leave, there lay his concubine with her hands on the threshold. He said, "Get up! Let's go!" But there was no answer, so he put her body on his donkey and took her home. When he got home, he took a knife and cut his concubine's body into twelve pieces. Then he sent one piece to each tribe throughout all the territory of Israel. Everyone who saw it said, "Such a thing has never been seen or done not since the day the Israelites came up out of Egypt. Think about it! Consider it! Tell us what to do!"

This story is a grievous account of how this girl suffered the mutilation and destruction of her physical body and spiritual man. What I find more heartbreaking is that this spirit of lawlessness reigns today and people in our society are still standing around, baffled and wondering what to do. Our daughters should be released to the man God has for them to be their husband, and until the husband comes, the Father is to be the priest, provider, and protector. If the Father is not there, this is where the church is called to serve. Perhaps we have forgotten that we were called to take care of the widows and orphans. James 1:27 says, "Religion that God our Father accepts as pure and faultless is this: to look after orphans and widows in their distress and to keep oneself from being polluted by the world."

> "RELIGION THAT GOD OUR FATHER ACCEPTS AS PURE AND FAULTLESS IS THIS: TO LOOK AFTER ORPHANS AND WIDOWS IN THEIR DISTRESS AND TO KEEP ONESELF FROM BEING POLLUTED BY THE WORLD."

Today, in American society where freedom prevails, our daughters are yet being taken. Statistics show that:

- One in five women and one in 71 men will be raped at some point in their lives.[9]

- 91 percent of the victims of rape and sexual assault are female, and 9 percent are male.[10]

- In 8 out of 10 cases of rape, the victim knew the person who sexually assaulted them.[11]

- One in four girls and one in six boys will be sexually

abused before they turn 18 years old.[12]

- 325,000 children are at risk of becoming victims of commercial child sexual exploitation each year.[13]

- The average age at which girls first become victims of prostitution is 12 to 14 years old, and the average age for boys is 11 to 13 years old.[14]

This is the reality we live in, and it begs the questions of where are the fathers and where is the church? The covering for these children is absent, and if the father is nowhere to be found, he cannot possibly be the priest, provider, and protector he should be. His daughters are being lured away by the enemy. For some, it is in his absence, and for others it is right before his eyes.

It says in the passage that she was unfaithful to him and she left him and went back to her father's house in Bethlehem, Judah. After she had been there four months, her husband went to her to persuade her to return . . . She took him into her father's house, and when her father saw him, he gladly welcomed him. Here we see that the daughter ran off, left this man, and fled to her father's house. Perhaps she was fleeing home because she had been unfaithful, and during that time you could be put to death for adultery. Consequently, she was seeking refuge in her father's home, but instead of her father surveying this man and his motives, by observing and asking questions, the father welcomed him and began feasting with him. Could he not see the despair in his daughter's eyes, or did the dowry mean so much more?

A GODLY FATHER

A father is to represent and provide protection to his

child, and in the passage she was running toward what was supposed to be a safe haven. The very thing she was running from, her father welcomed, as we see in verse 3. What happened to the fathers protecting their little girls? What happened to the spirit of discernment? This man turned his daughter back over into the hands of the enemy, and later she ends up in the hands of a second man who also refused to protect her and regarded her with little value. In the passage, we see that the perverse men went to the house, and the father pushed her out of the door like meat to fill their ravenous fleshly appetite.

This Levite had no regard for her and no concern for her well-being. He disgraced her by scattering her jewels among filthy dogs, who raped her all night long. And that is exactly what the enemy will do. He will rape you in the dark. He will rape you of your self-esteem and self-identity and leave you staggering, trying to find a grip on life. And what could be most appalling, at first take, is that at daybreak she went back to where the Levite was staying. How could she go back to the man who caused her this agonizing pain? Can you imagine it? She's been out in the open, raped all night long, probably covered in blood and dried semen, and with what little strength she has, she drags herself back to the man who threw her to the wolves to be eaten and destroyed. But how can you blame her? Her sense of self-worth was destroyed, she was disillusioned by the pain, and she found herself in the middle of nowhere in an unfamiliar land. Furthermore, Daddy allowed this Levite to take her and when she went back, and Daddy did nothing, she probably felt like she had nowhere else to go. Then not only did she die at the threshold, but he cut her up and scattered her across the land.

TOO MANY OF OUR DAUGHTERS ARE DYING ON THE THRESHOLD.

Too many of our daughters are dying on the threshold. *Webster's Dictionary* defines "threshold" as the point of entry or beginning, and so many of our daughters are dying at the point of entry of life.[15] Before they can get a foothold, their spirits are being crushed, their virginity snatched, their futures sabotaged. What happens to a girl when she is exposed to a man before she is exposed to righteousness? She loses herself before she can find herself, and she is left looking for the pieces of her heart that have been scattered to and fro.

THE MISSING VOICE

Where is the voice of the young woman? We never hear her speak. We hear the father's voice. We hear the Levite's voice. We even hear the stranger's voice. But the daughter's voice is silenced. Verse 30 testifies that people witnessed this heinous crime, but who intervened for her? They had so much to say about it, but no one was moved to action for the sake of justice. This Levite cut her up and scattered her parts across all of Israel. Who shall go reclaim her lost pieces and put them back together, that which he casted to the north, the south, the east, and west?

Where was the mother's voice in this situation? The voice of the nurturer, the breasted one, the one who hears her baby's whimper even in her deepest sleep. Where is she? The voice of the wise woman is nowhere to be found. If she were there she would have told her, "No, Daughter, he's not the one. Wait on your king."

For the mothers reading this text, you must wake up. Your daughters need you. They're grappling in the dark, looking for an anchor. They are stumbling and fumbling, trying to find the truth. If you leave her to figure out life alone, out of ignorance and immaturity, she may mess it up.

I believe that as a society we have failed to see how important a good mother and a good father is. In reading Judges chapter 19 with a modern-day perspective, I could not help but wonder where the parents were. We see the father, but he seems to be disengaged given that he releases his daughter to a man who ultimately killed her. Had he been more perceptive, would he have seen this Levite's violent tendencies and kept his daughter from him? Weak family structures can have a grave cost. This young girl from Bethlehem lost her life before it truly could begin because she lacked sound parenting.

Broken homes are like an epidemic, and the family structure as we know it—and how God intended it to be—stands in peril. In exploring why women are bent towards unhealthy relationships, we see that the root of this lies within family dynamics. I will define this more clearly for you, but the bottom line is this: future unhealthy relationships with men are birthed out of a past of unhealthy relationships with parents, particularly the father.

How a child grows up within a particular setting of family dynamics largely predicts the path they will take in life and how they will deal with their future spouse and children. There are vital things a mother and father each give their child separately that collectively define sound parenting. A father is to be the leader in the home. There are four ways in which he leads as a father: priest, protector, provider, and prophet. Let me define these four offices and provide a scriptural basis.

As the priest of the home, he goes to God on behalf of the children. He is constantly lifting them up before God and being the intercessor for his family. Job was a perfect example of this. Job 1:5 says, "And it was so, that when the days of their feasting were ended, Job sent and sanctified them [his children], and rose up early in the morning and offered burnt offerings according to the number of them all; for Job said, 'It may be that my sons have sinned and cursed God in their hearts.' This did Job continually."

Secondly, a father is to protect his home. He protects by establishing boundaries, regulation, and discipline. He authorizes and enforces discipline. Hebrews 12:7–11 reminds us that a father chastens out of love, and though it may hurt in the short term, it will produce the fruit of righteousness. Discipline protects a child by equipping them with the ability to make sound decisions and realize and weigh the consequences of their actions.

Thirdly, a father is to be the provider. God created man to work and bring forth as illustrated in Genesis when God created Adam and placed him in the Garden. Lastly, a father is to act as the prophet in the home. He is to provide instruction and training in the Word of God. He is to proclaim to his family, "Thus says the Lord." This is where vision and direction for the family comes from. Deuteronomy 11:18–20 instructs with great passion to teach the children the command of God. To teach them when they rise up for the day, wind down for the night, when they sit, and when they walk. And in fact, be so bold to write the command of God on the doorposts of the home! This passage is communicating that it is so important for the Word of God to be the first and last thing entering the ear gate of your child. It is so important for them to walk in the Word and be submerged in it and for them to see the Word alive in the home. It should become their lifestyle, because you have made the presence of God "normal" to them. It simply should be apart of everyday life. The father must be bold and stand firm just like Joshua and proclaim, "As for me and my house, we will serve the Lord!"[16]

IT SHOULD BECOME THEIR LIFESTYLE, BECAUSE YOU HAVE MADE THE PRESENCE OF GOD "NORMAL" TO THEM.

On the other hand, the mother is to be the helpmeet for the father. The Lord said very clearly in Genesis 2:18, "It is not good that man should be alone. I will make him a helper suitable for him." Woman was created to be a companion and a helper to fulfill God's purpose. She is to carry out the vision that the father provides, and they must be on one accord with each other. The mother is also to be the manager of the home and the nurturer of the family. Proverbs 31:10–31 so eloquently paints the picture of a virtuous wife: "She rises up while it is yet night and gives food to her household . . . She is not afraid of the snow for her household, for all her household are clothed with scarlet . . . She looks well to the ways of her household, and does not eat the bread of idleness." It is clear that a virtuous wife attends to the needs of her family and home without hesitation and does so gracefully.

This is the framework for an established godly home. This is the situation in which the children arise and call her blessed.[17] But when there is a breakdown in the family structure and there are missing elements, a child cannot grow up to utter such an honorable proverb. Colossians 3:21 says, "Fathers, do not embitter your children, or they will become discouraged." This resembles more of the reality we share. Children are embittered because fathers are gone and not walking in their rightful place, and mom is left to fill the shoes of daddy. But, guess what? Her feet are too small! She does not have the capacity or makeup to father her children, and her children are distracted by her shortcomings in trying to nurture, manage, and be the provider in the home. She is trying to fill their bellies when their spirits are dying of hunger. She is trying to put a roof over their heads when they have little foundation to stand on. If she could do it all, God would not have created the man *and* woman to be the foundation of the family unit. In everything God does, it has a purpose and a place.

Yet this is the story of so many children born into single-family homes. Statistics show that 35 percent of all children under eighteen years of age live in a single parent household, and 66 percent and 42 percent of African American and Hispanic children, respectively, are growing up in single parent households. Yet, it is these same fatherless homes that accounts for 63 percent of youth suicides, 90 percent of homeless/runaway children, 85 percent of children with behavior problems, 71 percent of high school dropouts, 85 percent of youths in prison, and well over 50 percent of teen mothers. These are national statistics; it is a human condition that crosses all cultural lines.[18]

In the text we examined in Judges 19, we saw how the father failed that young unwedded girl and did not provide her what she needed to be successful. We see that she left and went back to her father's house in Bethlehem Judah. Bethlehem means "house of bread," and she went back because she was hungry. Not necessarily that she could be filled, but because she was hungry. Nowhere in the passage do you read of her eating. Multiple times it refers to the Levite and her father eating.

When a woman was never fed by her father, her hunger will drive her into the arms of a man, and nine times out of ten it will be the wrong man, because in her brokenness her judgment is skewed. This is the very reason we must have a relationship with God, because where there is lack He will fill every void. Even in the midst of not being fed by your biological father, God says to come and feed from the bread of heaven, where you'll want no more.[19] He says to drink of the living water where you'll never thirst again. God can give you all that you've been missing.[20] You don't have to walk around broken and hungry, because if you don't feed of God, nothing will be able to satiate your hunger and quench your thirst.

That which a father is to give is unique by design and nothing can substitute it, and nothing can replace it. The only one who can fill that place, if there is a void, is God Himself. Anybody else will always come up short. Often it

> THAT WHICH A FATHER IS TO GIVE IS UNIQUE BY DESIGN AND NOTHING CAN SUBSTITUTE IT, AND NOTHING CAN REPLACE IT.

is an affirmation of who you are and a feeling of security that is so desperately desired. That desire and need for security includes protection, an unfailing unconditional love, and a rested place secure and shielded from the pressures of the world and the works of darkness. Simply put, a woman just wants to know that it is all right. That it's all right to lay her head down. That it's all right to love. That her heart is all right in the hands that it has been placed. She wants to be free from being afraid.

For this young Bethlehem girl, there was no mother's voice, so she went away with a man she may have thought could provide the security she longed for. A place of rest, away from her fears. Nonetheless, the story ends that she dies in a fallen position with her hands on the threshold. She was reaching. She died reaching for help. Many women are reaching for help and some are unseen, and others are ignored. They are dying at the threshold, but truly wanting help to get up and walk in freedom if someone would just show them the way.

This is not something to just pray about and forget. We are the hands and feet of Jesus and it takes commitment, sacrifice, involvement, and new thinking on our parts. Jeremiah 29:11 says, 'For I know the plans I have for you,' declares the LORD, plans to prosper you and not to harm you, plans to give you a hope and a future.'" The amazing thing is that God does not stop there! In verses 12–14, God says, 'Then you will call upon me and come and pray to me and I will listen to you. You will seek me and find me when you seek me with all your heart. I will be found by you' declares the LORD, 'and will bring you back from captivity. I will gather you from all the nations and places where I have banished you' declares the LORD, 'and will bring you back to the place from which I carried you into exile."'

When we go back to our God wholeheartedly, neither "playing church" nor being "religious," but seeking Him wholeheartedly, He will bring forth the restoration. He'll gather our minds to be sound and not scattered. He'll gather our homes and families to be what He intended it to be and not scattered. He'll gather the denominations to be one church, one body, and not scattered. God is looking for a church, a people, a generation that will seek His face. "Lift up your heads oh ye gates and the King of Glory shall come in."[21] My Sisters, let the King of glory come in and not another one of us will die at the threshold.

Beyond the Threshold,
Jennifer

Questions TO PONDER AND DISCUSS

1. Are there things in your past that you need to let go of or deal with, that keep causing recurring trouble in your life?

2. How have your upbringing and childhood experiences shaped your outlook on yourself and marriage?

3. Are there people in your life you need to forgive, so that you can move forward?

4. Are you struggling with something incessantly? Do you see patterns of it in your family? If so, what do you think the root of it is?

5. How was your father a protector, provider, priest, and prophet in the home? Are there roles he did not fulfill? If so, which ones and how do you think it affected you?

6. Was your mom a nurturer, manager of the home, and helpmeet to your dad? How did she fulfill this role or not, and how do you think this impacted your life?

A *Prayer* TO PRAY

Dear Lord, I am looking for your healing and restoration power to be manifested in my life. My heart is heavy with choices and mistakes made in the past. Sometimes tears flow from me, both those seen and others only from my heart. Your Word says to me in Psalms 138 that when I cried out to you, you heard me, and answered me. You made me bold with strength and though I walk in the midst of trouble you revive my life! You will stretch out your hand against the wrath of my enemies, and your right hand saves me! You promised, Lord, that you will perfect that which concerns me. Your mercy, oh Lord, endures forever, and I know that you will not forsake the work of your hands. Lord, you are my portion, my present help, and in You there is no lack. Bread of heaven, feed me. Feed me until I want no more. Quench my thirst, Father, and satiate my hunger. I'm desperate for you. Renew me again and make me over. You said the old man has passed away and I am a new creature, so I declare my past this day is dead and has no power over me. My future is glorious and I will walk therein.

In Jesus' Name I pray, Amen.

Success is not final, failure is not fatal:
it is the courage to continue that counts.

WINSTON CHURCHILL

Letter #3:

TO EDEN I GO

My Beloved Sister,

I know we have uncovered some hard truths. The material in Letter #2 was quite heavy, but these are necessary issues to expose and discuss when we are talking about being all that God created us to be. Often, our struggles in our flesh are birthed from events from our childhood or the absence of something fundamental. Sin is the result of the enemy perverting a legitimate desire.[22] As humans we have basic needs of shelter, security, love, and acceptance. It is the absence of the need being met that makes one vulnerable to meet the need in an illegitimate way. Just think about it. People steal because they are hungry or in need of something like transportation, housing, or money. People commit adultery and fornicate because of the desire for acceptance, security, and or love. Sin is the illegitimate way of meeting a legitimate need. This is why the Bible tells us, "Be not entangled again with the yoke of bondage

> SIN IS THE ILLEGITIMATE WAY OF MEETING A LEGITIMATE NEED.

and to lay aside every weight and sin that so easily beset us."[23] It so easily besets us because it is the illusion of the fulfillment of a particular need that our soul longs for. It is common, familiar, comfortable, or even pleasurable for the moment, but it is deceptive because it never really meets that need. Sin is the counterfeit solution, and when sin grows up, it gives birth to death. It is the death of that illusion or fantasy and reality, and then its real consequences begin to unfold.

Thus, it is important to analyze the past, so the past will not live in our future. You must understand what made you who you are, how your environment shaped you, what things you need to unlearn and abandon, and what things you need to embrace and challenge yourself with. When you can understand why you have been bent towards certain carnal behaviors and poor choices, you will then know how to deal with yourself, what to pray for, what to flee from, and what to seek after.

We explored single parent homes and absent fathers in the previous letter. Absent fathers and single parent homes are the leading reasons women become sexually promiscuous, develop unhealthy relationships, and often fail in marriage. However, these are not the only dynamics that can cause future unhealthy relationships. There are other dynamics like: mom leading the family and dad having a poor work ethic, dad working too much, both mom and dad working too much, unmarried cohabitating parents and the mixed messages that arrangement sends about commitment, abuse between parents whether married or unmarried, or just plain emotional disengagement. All these things can cause a child to grow up and not be able to deal with someone of the opposite sex in a healthy manner and build lasting substantial relationships with people. Whenever a parent is not exemplifying the characteristics completely of what we mentioned in the previous letter of what makes a family healthy then that child is missing a vital element in their development. Specifically, for daughters, they do not learn to grow as women of wisdom and, ultimately they can lack the understanding of what truly makes a man a man of God and what it means to relate to one.

Secondly, emotional disengagement on either part of the parents can be just as damaging as the parent's absence. A daughter needs to be actively taught, trained, conversed with, and shown love and affection daily. The lack of an emotional bond can cause a wall to be erected between the child and the parent. A girl does not necessarily have to become promiscuous, but issues with temperament, self-esteem, excessive shyness, sense of being lost, loss of ambition, loneliness, or curiosities towards other vices can arise.

The ideas of a working mother and a single parent have become such cultural norms that the sense of "independence" has surged amongst women. This was largely embraced during the feminist movement and has become accepted in society. Women have gone from one extreme to the other, but no matter how society evolves, God's Word never changes. God's Word is infallible and timeless, and His design for the family is guaranteed for success. This is not

> GOD'S WORD IS INFALLIBLE AND TIMELESS, AND HIS DESIGN FOR THE FAMILY IS GUARANTEED FOR SUCCESS.

JENNIFER IMEDIEGWU

to say that two working parents are automatically outside of God's will, but it is clearly stated in the Bible as to what the role of each parent should be. The context in which that is fulfilled will vary for each family.

Getting back to the topic of sin, I would like to point out that the lack of a parent fulfilling their role is the exercise of man and woman's original sin. When a father is not being the priest, provider, protector, and prophet in his home, it is a manifestation of his old Adamic nature and the sin of irresponsibility, just as we saw in the beginning of time. God gave Adam the vision and instruction to not eat of the Tree of the Knowledge of God and Evil. It was his neglect of adhering to this instruction that caused him to fail as being the protector and provider of his home. Thus, his wife Eve was deceived.²⁴

However, on the flipside Eve knew what God said to Adam, because she quoted it back to the devil, yet she stepped out in her own will and desire and ate of what was forbidden. Her independence caused her to shirk her responsibility of being the helpmeet: one to help fulfill the vision of her husband and have no private agenda. Woman's original sin was, in fact, independence. Her flesh was roused, and she acted independent of her husband's authority, which happened to be the most destructive act of mankind. If God says His divine order is for man to be the head and the woman is to submit to him in everything, and this model of submission precisely implemented brings forth man and woman's ability to walk in dominion, then we must realize that doing the contrary breeds the contrary. Thus, walking in rebellion results in bondage. The fact that Eve stepped out of divine order meant things could only become more and more

60

destructive. The Bible says one is dragged away by desire, and desire becomes sin, and when sin is full grown it gives birth to death.[25] Her own desires took her captive and drug her into bondage. This rebellious spirit, if not driven out, is transferred to the children as we see with Eve's son, Cain. God warned Cain that sin was crouching at the door if he did not do well. In utter denial of this revelation, Cain rebelled and slew his brother and was driven from the presence of the Lord.[26] This is the result of a woman stepping out of divine order, walking in independence, void of any covering. The fruit she bears is corrupt, when sin reigns.

In my opinion, a modern-day example of this is the correlation of the feminist movement and divorce rates. Certainly, there were positive aspects of the movement and the much-deserved liberation of women with regards to property ownership, earnings, and opportunities outside of the home. But no extreme is ever healthy, and that is what we have seen in recent times with very radical expressions of freedom. The more women have embraced this false sense of independence, without boundaries, it bears reason to why marriages have fallen apart even more. This is the cost of sin. This picture seems to be quite devastating. The very thing that caused the destruction of mankind in the beginning still rings true in the present time. Surely it seems hopeless. Adam and Eve were banished from the Garden, and to make sure they did not get back, God placed fiery blazing cherubim to guard it. They were removed from the perfect order and fellowship with God and banished into chaos having to fend for themselves. This chaos seems familiar with our present-day version of irresponsible men and independent women not knowing how to communicate, understand, or live at peace and in love with one another.

Can we ever get back to the Garden of Eden, the state of harmony between man and woman walking in intimate fellowship with God? Clearly, that is what they had. God walked amongst Adam and Eve in the Garden, and they were naked. This nakedness exemplifies there were no barriers, there was total intimacy, honesty, and transparency. How sweet and peaceful this sounds. It was something too precious to be lost and God knew it. Though, Adam and Eve corrupted God's perfect creation, the love God had for us caused him to restore it. This is what Jesus Christ came for. What Adam destroyed, Jesus Christ re-established. Romans 5:17 says, "For if, because of one man's trespass, death reigned through that one man, much more will those who receive the abundance of grace and the free gift of righteousness reign in life through the one man, Jesus Christ."

> THIS IS WHAT JESUS CHRIST CAME FOR. WHAT ADAM DESTROYED, JESUS CHRIST RE-ESTABLISHED.

This righteousness comes from God through faith in Jesus Christ for all who believe, and we are justified freely by His grace through the redemption we receive through Him (Rom. 3:22–24). This is the way back. Jesus said, "I am the way and the truth and the life. No one comes to the Father except through me."[27] We can't get to the Father except through Him. He's like the blazing cherubim that once stood between God and man. Only this time, there is an open door, and it is the faith in Jesus that He is our Lord and Savior and that He was the sacrifice of atonement that redeemed us from eternal death and damnation. Once we enter true fellowship with God through Christ, restoration will take place in our spiritual lives and natural lives. It is then that we can be the men and women God created us to be and fulfill our potential as we were created in His image. The curse and bondage of sin from our forefathers and ourselves has been broken at the cross, and we are released from the demonic hold of the enemy simply by receiving salvation.

Looking into your past and even your present, you may see patterns and may now be able to connect the dots and understand why certain actions were taken. But it is not for you to lay blame on someone, it is for you to walk in deliverance and live the abundant life Christ died for you to have. My Sister, if you do this you will be making a life-changing decision. Walk in faith and believe what you have received. You are a new creature and the old has passed away. Forget those things that are behind you and press forward to obtain that for which Christ took hold of you.[28]

As I press,
Jennifer

Questions TO PONDER AND DISCUSS

1. Is there something standing between you and God? Is it a career? Money? A certain lifestyle? A particular habit? How has this impacted your relationship with God and your future goals?

2. How can we exercise independence in a way that glorifies God?

3. What about submission scares you? What does God's Word say about submission? See First Peter 3:1–7; James 4:1–10.

A *Prayer* TO PRAY

Lord, here I am at the threshold in need of you. I want a new beginning, and I need a new start. I realize that things in my past have hindered my progress and clouded my understanding of who you created me to be. But this day, I ask for you to give me the mind of Christ and the direction of your Holy Spirit to walk in your perfect will. I forgive those who harmed me. I bless those who curse me. I release those for holding me captive by their ignorance. And now, God, I surrender myself to you completely, withholding nothing. I accept Jesus Christ as my Lord and Savior and I ask that you make me whole, complete, and lacking no good thing. Every void is cancelled in the name of Jesus. My hunger and thirst are for you alone, that which is pure, holy, not carnal, and nondestructive. Wash me in your blood, renew a right spirit within me, give me a heart submitted to you, O God. You are my strong tower, my Prince of Peace, my anchor in the time of trouble, my present help, and the lover of my soul. Come in to me Father. Fill me with your spirit and restore to my life the glory of Eden where your presence and harmony resides. I want to do your will. Master me and be Lord over me; be my strength and my Redeemer.

In Jesus' name I pray, Amen.

Where we are met with cynicism and doubts and those who tell us that we can't, we will respond with that timeless creed that sums up the spirit of a people: Yes, we can!

PRESIDENT BARACK OBAMA

Letter #4:

DAUGHTERS OF DESTINY

My Beloved Sister,

Your stilettos are now firmly placed on the path to your destiny. The restoration of Eden is yours to have and I encourage you to fiercely follow after it. When we set our eyes on God and fall in love with the things of God, in due season, we will find ourselves smack-dab in the middle of our purpose. The Lord created us in His image, and the closer we draw to Him, the clearer the image becomes. He is the source of the light needed to illuminate who we are and what we were created to be. You see, God has double vision; He can see us in the present and in the future. He can see us as we are and, simultaneously, see the manifestation of our potential. The closer we get to Him, the less we will focus on our faults and failures, but we will begin to see more and more of what God created us to be and do. The closer we get to

HE CAN SEE US AS WE ARE AND, SIMULTANEOUSLY, SEE THE MANIFESTATION OF OUR POTENTIAL.

Him, the closer we are to achieving the oneness He so long desired, and with that comes the power *to become.* We were created in His image. We were created to be like Him, and the more we tap into this divine nature, the more we are empowered to produce and walk in dominion here in the earthly realm.

The matters of our destiny become so simple when we put God into the equation. He said, "Seek first His kingdom and His righteousness and *all* these things shall be added unto you."[29] He said, "Delight yourself in me and I will give you the desires of your heart."[30] He said, "For I know the plans I have for you, plans to prosper you, not to harm you, to give you a hope, and an expected end."[31] Do you get it? He has the answer! He knows the plans for your life and if you get to know the one who has the top secret He'll share it with you after a while.[32] Certainly you can't manipulate God; nor is He Santa Claus, where you can jump up onto his knee and tell Him all the things you want for Christmas and then run away. He will test and prove what is in your heart before ushering you into the Promised Land. After He knows that you plan to stick around for the long haul and that you truly are in love with Him, then He will begin to reveal the matters of His heart, which are the answers you have so desperately and aimlessly sought after before finding Him.

Finding your life's purpose is really that simple. You can take all the courses and personality quizzes in the world, and use career match services, but those things will only take you so far. They may point you in the direction of your interests or even highlight your strengths and gifts. But God is the only one who can put it all together and order your steps to fulfill that which you were created for *using* those interests, strengths, and gifts. God helps us make sense of us. He connects the dots and provides meaning. Making our relationship with God the most supreme relationship and our life's priority places all other things into perspective and provides meaning and understanding to life's circumstances and relationships. This must be our focus if we are to lead the most satisfying and potential-maximizing life.

I would like to share a scriptural revelation the Lord gave me as I was seeking Him for direction concerning my own life's destiny. In the book of Joshua we find the Lord's command of Him to lead the Israelites into the Promised Land. In Joshua chapter 1 God tells Joshua four times in that chapter alone to be strong and courageous. The Lord knew what challenges Joshua would face ahead, and He felt it was necessary to remind Him several times as to seal in its importance. The one thing that is important to know about destiny is that it is bigger than you and you cannot do it alone. Anything that you can do in your own strength is never the pinnacle of what God has for you or created you for. God's plans for your life is to stretch you, cause you to come to the end of yourself, and lean totally on Him to get the job done. There is no other way and God knows it. That is why it is no mistake that He tells Joshua a whopping four times to be strong and courageous! Furthermore, He gives Joshua a profound nugget. He says to him, "Do not let this book of the law depart from your mouth, meditate on it day and night, so that you may be careful

> FOLLOW THE WORD AND YOU WILL FOLLOW LIFE'S SUCCESS.

to do everything written in it. Then you will be prosperous and successful." Doesn't this sound familiar? Simply stated, follow the Word and you will follow life's success.

As Joshua and the Israelites continued on their journey, the Lord promised that if the ark of the covenant went ahead of them, when the priests set foot into the Jordan River carrying the ark, the sea would back up. The Scriptures said that the priests who carried the ark of the covenant of the Lord stood firm on dry ground in the middle of the Jordan River while *all* of Israel passed by crossing on dry ground. This is so amazing to me, and it is a vivid reminder for us to allow God to be in the middle of our situations. The Lord parted a body of water to ease their transition. God makes life so much easier for us if we let Him. The story says that they stood firm on dry ground. This could only be God's doing. Can't you imagine it, the river standing back, and it would be nothing but wet, sandy earth? However, when God is present, He makes our footing sure and even performs supernatural acts the human mind cannot fathom.

When Joshua and the Israelites came to a certain point in their journey, He stopped feeding them manna and allowed them to eat the produce from Canaan. Literally it was the day after they ate the food from Canaan that the manna stopped. You see, what sustained you previously will be inadequate for where God is taking you. It will be replaced with something greater, and He will allow you to taste of it! Those sweet moments dropped into our lives sparingly and unexpectedly are what keeps us encouraged and reminded of what is to come. It gives us that staying power to press through when times get tough, because you have tasted of what is on the other side and you know it is worth all the sweat and every tear it takes to get there.

The Israelites began to eat of Canaan's produce even before they took Jericho! But what we can't do when God gives us these treats is get off track, get lazy, and start slacking. When the Israelites got to Jericho, the Lord gave them clear directions: He said that the city and all that is in it are to be devoted to the Lord. They were to take nothing, not a single thing! The Lord left no wiggle room, yet someone in the camp could not resist the temptation. Achan took some of the devoted things like gold and bronze articles, and because of Achan's choice, the Lord's anger burned against Israel.

The story of Achan has a twofold revelation to me. First, we must be careful of who we have in our camp with us. Whomever you are tied to, their actions will affect how far you will go. Their mistakes can hinder your progress and be a liability you cannot afford to carry. Secondly, Achan reminds me of our flesh, while Joshua reminds me of our spirit. Achan wanted what he wanted right then and there. He did not want to wait. Furthermore, his guilt caused him to go bury it in his tent. How much could he really enjoy the gold and silver buried in the ground? Not much, but there is some inkling of pleasure to know you have it that is gratifying to the flesh. Paul said, what benefit did you reap for the things of which you are now ashamed? There is no benefit. It is a short-lived pleasure to go after things prematurely, and it may come at a cost you thought was smaller when blinded by the glitter. You get so little, but you lose so much. It simply is not worth what you sacrifice for the thrill. Achan and all his possessions, livestock, and family were stoned and burned. He could have enjoyed the fruits of God's promises had he just waited on the timing of God. Do you see that our decisions affect those we are connected to? His family was stoned and burned for *his* decisions and greed.

At the start of this downturn, Joshua and the Israelites began to lose battles, and he fell facedown, pleading with God as to why God had forsaken them. He stayed there all night, and God yet was not impressed with his grief. The Lord's voice thundered like an upset Father, and He told him to get up! This was not the time for worship; it was the time for cleaning. There is a time and place for everything, and at this point God was not looking for sacrifice. He precisely told Joshua that Israel had sinned and until whatever was devoted to destruction that was among them was destroyed, He would not be with them. It was a clear ultimatum: "If you want me, clean yourself up!"

So often our spirits are crying out to God, like Joshua, about the chaos in our lives and especially when you know God promised you something, but it seems like the exact opposite is happening. However, that may very well be the time God is saying get up and dust yourself off. We must continually self evaluate: "Am I letting Achan ruin things in the camp and then burying it?"

We cannot go after things prematurely, nor can we harbor sin in our lives—just like David said his bones withered and body ached when he let sin go unconfessed.[33] Sin festers and devours whatever it has preyed upon, if left uncast. Sin is the first thing that can hold us back from fulfilling our destiny. However, a second issue that can be just as stagnating is: failing to believe what God said and what He has promised. It is one thing to hear God, but the greater thing is to hold fast to the revelation. If you forget what God said, you will go looking in the wrong place for solutions and answers; or worse, when the answer is right before you, you won't even grasp it because you're not in tune to see it.

Luke 24 shares with us the story of Jesus' disciples after His ascension. They did not believe the testimony of the women, nor the angels, that Jesus had indeed rose, and it was for that reason alone that His tomb was empty. Can't you recall Jesus telling them countless times these very events would happen? The prophets foretold this, and the law of Moses was a record of his death, burial, and resurrection that was to come. We cannot walk so close to Jesus and His words yet not become living to us. They should not have been shocked whatsoever. Their spirits should have leaped with confirmation at the testimony just as Elizabeth's babe leapt when she saw Mary, the mother of Jesus.

> WE CANNOT WALK SO CLOSE TO JESUS AND HIS WORDS YET NOT BECOME LIVING TO US.

Perhaps they doubted the testimony because of all the people Jesus could have appeared to, He appeared to Mary, the sister of Martha? With this line of thinking, we must remind ourselves that Jesus is no respecter of person and He sees only the heart. Jesus delivered Mary and some other women from demons and diseases, and from that day forward they followed closely to Him to not only meet His needs, but to *know* Him. When Jesus came to stay in the house of Martha and Mary, Martha busied herself with housework to impress Jesus, but it was Mary who sat at His feet to listen to the words flowing from His lips. Martha, distracted by the preparations for Jesus, didn't have time to get close to Him in an intimate way. Jesus even said that Mary chose what was better. He isn't impressed with the fanfare; He just wants us to draw close to Him and sit at His feet. Mary was faithful, and she shared herself with Jesus. She anointed Him with oil that was very precious and worth nearly a year's wages, and she let down her hair to wipe His feet. How humbling of herself to go against custom to show her loyalty and honor for her king. It was an act of courage and intimacy, because it was against Jewish custom to let one's hair down in public. It was something to be done privately, in one's own closed chambers. However, she knew she had to seize every moment she had with Jesus; there simply was no time to waste. If it meant being in public, only to mentally block out the presence of others, then that was what she was willing to do because she knew the end was drawing near and the Jesus she knew on earth would soon be no more. She may not have fully understood the coming of the Holy Spirit and Jesus' second coming, but she knew that if there was a moment she could steal away with Jesus, it was worth getting and giving all she could and not leave His presence having not tapped in.

Let us go back to the initial question of why the disciples doubted the testimony. A more substantive explanation to this doubt lies in the fact that they very well could have walked with Jesus, yet their ears, eyes, and hearts were not open to completely perceive the depth of Jesus' ministry. At this point, when Jesus reappeared to them after his death, the disciples had not come to the ends of themselves. We cannot really perceive the nature of God and Him fully when our flesh is yet in the way.

During Jesus' ministry it was the time for the disciples to watch, learn, and follow. This was a season of mentoring and preparation for the mandate God had placed on their lives. Mark 9 shares with us that a man brought his child to the disciples and they could not heal him. This is because their time had not come to perform miracles; they were yet in training. One thing we must realize about God is that He does not call us and then immediately release us to do the work for which He ultimately called us. Just as the Israelites had to go through a time of testing for God to prove what was in their hearts to determine whether they could handle the next level or not, He did the same thing with the disciples. With the Israelites, God wanted to make sure that when they made it to Canaan they would not forget who brought them there. He said that if you forget the Lord your God, then you'll have the audacity to say it was your hands that got you this wealth, but it is He who gives you the power to produce wealth.[34]

The disciples had to be grounded and rooted in their understanding that it was the Lord's kingdom they would be establishing on the earth, not their own. They had to become mature enough to not abuse the power they would be given, especially when Jesus said that greater signs would follow. They were to do what Jesus did and more, but they had to be at a point where they had fully absorbed what Jesus had previously taught them—that no servant is greater than his master. Just as it was God that gave the people of Israel the power to produce wealth, once again it was the power of God within the disciples to perform miracles and establish the kingdom of God and make disciples of all nations.

When Jesus was on earth, after He had risen, He gave them some last instructions. He made it clear that they were to wait on the filling of the Holy Spirit before they went out to Jerusalem to minister. When Jesus ascended, they were not to break out into the streets running their mouths, but they would know the time had come when the power of God came upon them.[35]

From the time of Jesus calling the disciples to the time of them being sent out into the world was a period of three and a half years. Once again, God never calls and immediately releases! Another demonstration of God doing this is with Abraham. When Abraham was first called he was seventy-five years old, but it was not until he was one hundred years old that Isaac finally came! God does not do this to lead us on and tease us, but it is in our best interest we are adequately prepared to receive His blessings. The truth of the matter, is that God's will is so outstanding, so mind-blowing that He doesn't want the greediness and selfishness of our flesh to ruin it. God loves us so much that He doesn't want us to self-destruct. So the period of

GOD LOVES US SO MUCH THAT HE DOESN'T WANT US TO SELF-DESTRUCT.

testing and teaching He takes us through is to crucify our flesh and for us to really be able to take up our lives in Him. Don't you think that if the disciples were called and sent out immediately, they would have gotten beaten up and swallowed up by the world and probably would have just quit and went back to their simple lives of fishing? God's plan is extremely beautiful and the most satisfying, yet it is not the easiest thing we could be spending our lives doing. So that's reason number three He takes us through this period of preparation—to build within us the spiritual stamina to stay the course. Furthermore, it is for us to grow in the knowledge of Him *and* in love with Him that we'll come to a point that our deepest longing is for His will and not our will.

During the period of preparation, the heat gets turned up. This isn't for those who just want a handout from God like He's Santa Claus. This preparation separates the sheep from the goats. Jesus said that only He who does the will of my Father will enter the kingdom of heaven. Matthew 7 says there will be many who say, "Lord, Lord we prophesied in your name, and cast out demons in your name." Yet these are the ones who Jesus will tell, "Depart from me you evildoers, I never knew you."

Christ is not interested in us playing church and going through the motions when it is convenient and socially acceptable. He wants us to be like Mary and let our hair down. He wants us to be Christians who are committed through rain or sunshine, popularity or unpopularity, status quo or going against the grain. This is what gives us the power to become! When Christ fed the five thousand, He had a major following after that, because they were getting freebies and it felt good! However, when He began to teach the Word, the powerful Word sharper than a two-edge sword, and it pierced through their flesh to their very souls, many became uncomfortable and turned angry and could not stand the heavy teaching. Nonetheless, Jesus was not shaken by this ridicule and uproar. In response, He said, "This is why I told you that no one can come to me unless the Father has enabled him."

We cannot do the will of God in our flesh; it is impossible because the flesh does not know God, it is hostile toward God, and it does not submit to God's law, nor can it do so.[36] But, it is through our spirit that we can tap into the nature of God, and it is the spirit of Christ in us that makes our spirits alive. Those who are led by the spirit of God are sons of God and co-heirs with Christ, and if indeed we share in His sufferings, we may also share in His glory.[37]

When the disciples finally went out into the world, they went out with power. The period of preparation gave them what they needed for what they would face ahead. The same disciples who could do nothing for the boy bound by a demon were the same disciples who walked with great power and authority, healing the sick, opening blind eyes, raising the lame, saving souls, and driving out demons when it was God's timing. You see, when God puts his hand on our five loaves and two fish, He takes what was for our comfortable consumption and transforms our character and enlarges our capacity to bless and influence others greatly beyond our own natural capabilities for the purpose alone to glorify Him, our Father in heaven.

My Sisters, this is what God is calling for. This kind of depth is a depth that goes beyond the veil and presses in to the Holies of Holies. The Lord says He seeks a worshipper. Anybody can praise God; be an usher, help kids in church, or sing in the choir, but remember that worship is intimate. You must really know God to be able to enter into worship. Praise says, "Thank you for the bread you put on my table" but worship says, "You are the true and living bread. Feed me from heaven until I want no more." A worshipper is one who is willing to dig deep, to lay down their life, to say, "Not my will, but your will be done."

This separates the sheep from the goats, the wannabes from the real D.I.V.A.S, who are **D**ivinely **I**ntellectual and **V**irtuously **A**cclaimed. My Sisters, I want you to know that at this very moment you are knocking at the door of your destiny. You are a daughter of destiny and she is a daughter submitted to her King. The disciples had to wait for Jesus to be glorified until they received the power of the Holy Spirit, but the Holy Spirit has been given and our Lord has been glorified so the fulfillment of our destiny is not a waiting dependent on the providence of God, but it is a waiting dependent on our own spiritual fitness. You cannot go out into the world and be effective until God has done in you what He needs to do. Everything you need to do the will of God is already housed in you, but everything you need to activate God's will is hidden in Him. Seek out the King. Submit to Him. Enter into his royal courts and sit at His feet to receive. The King is waiting.

> YOU ARE A DAUGHTER OF DESTINY AND SHE IS A DAUGHTER SUBMITTED TO HER KING.

At His feet,
Jennifer

Questions TO PONDER AND DISCUSS

1. What are some goals you have that you truly believe God gave you? Are you following through on them? If not, how can you do better?

2. What keeps you from that Mary—like commitment, to "let your hair down" and care only about being at the feet of Jesus? Is it the busyness of life? Kids? Work? Chores?

3. Are there any "Achans" in your life? How can you eliminate the "Achans" and increase the Joshua confidence and courage?

4. How is God training you? What is He equipping you for?

A *Prayer* TO PRAY

Dear Lord,

You are an amazing God. You are all powerful. You are all-knowing. You are the all-sufficient one, El Shaddai. Father, you know the end from the beginning and you know everything about me. Father, I thank you that you are a covenant-keeping God. You are a God that cannot lie, so what you have said in your Word about me *has* to come to pass. Father, I believe my future is blessed and that I am aligned with your will for my destiny to unfold.

Father, please give me the heart of Mary, to press in and want you more than anything. Please give me the courage of Joshua, to stay the course to my promised land. Lord, please remove the Achans around me and the Achan in me, that nobody and nothing will hinder me from your promises. Lastly, Lord, I pray that you give me the anointing you gave your disciples to do even greater things in your name that are bigger than I can imagine and bigger than what I could ever do on my own.

Lord, I trust you for provision, that you will provide the means by which the vision shall be realized. I hold fast to my faith and I channel my gifts, energy, and resources in the direction of fulfilling the dreams you have placed in me.

In Jesus' Mighty Name,
Amen.

One of the greatest values of mentors is the ability to see ahead what others cannot see and to help them navigate a course to their destination.

JOHN C. MAXWELL

Letter #5:

AT HER FEET I SUPPED

My Beloved Sister,

We have talked extensively about going deeper in God. Our healing from the past and the clarity of our future is at the foot of the cross. However, we can't do life by ourselves. Having a robust life is not only about the vertical relationship we have with our Lord, but the horizontal relationships we have with others are equally important. When our horizontal relationships are healthy and Spirit-filled, God can use these relationships to help us reach our destiny.

Mentors are especially important, because these are people who have travelled the road ahead. They are where you want to be and can offer insight and encouragement along the way. Finding a mentor may be somewhat difficult. However, the most important thing to do is to allow it to be strategically designed by God as a divine appointment. Uncontrolled desperation can lead you into the hands of a crafty woman who feasts on vulnerable women.

If you think there is someone God has put in your

path, observe her before approaching her. Ask yourself these questions:

- Is she a praying woman?
- Is she submitted to her own husband?
- Does her children rise up and call her blessed?
- Is she building her home with her hands and positioning her husband to be at the city gate, instead of going ahead of him to her own seat?
- Is she a woman of nobility, integrity, and excellence?
- Is she a woman of wisdom? The heavenly wisdom that is first pure, peace seeking, considerate, submissive, and righteous?
- Is she modest or defined by materialism?
- Is she selfless, yet self-confident?
- Is she humble, yet walking in holy boldness?

Certainly, these are many questions, but they are all important to consider. It is imperative that you measure her against the Word of God according to what God says a holy woman is. Other women can be educational or professional mentors. They can show you how to write a thesis or find employment. However, when it comes to life, love, destiny, purpose, and the timing of all these things, such a mentor must be a woman who is trustworthy and filled with the Holy Spirit.

I recall going to a new church at the age of fifteen, and I took a liking to the pastor's wife. She was pretty, well dressed, and gentle as a dove. But that is not what I found to be most captivating. It was the beauty and depth of her spirit that was so amazing that as a budding young woman I could not help but watch her. I observed her for two years before concluding she was surely authentic.

I remember the day I approached her. I was lost in a web of sin but full of potential and needed someone to be a pillar in my life. I nervously asked with great expectation, "Can I get under your wings? Can I get at your feet and glean wisdom and soak up some of your essence?" I will never forget her warm smile and touch of love as she embraced me and said unreservedly, "Yes!" I cried profusely in her bosom. It was like the bolted latch on my heart was ripped away and the matters of my heart went rushing into this new place of refuge. She walked with me hand in hand into womanhood. She helped develop me into the person God was calling me to be. She gave me the answer to life's reverberating questions of, Who am I, what is my purpose, and what is my destiny? I can yet hear her sweet voice with a slight raspiness say, "Daughter, just fall in love with Jesus!"

"CAN I GET UNDER YOUR WINGS? CAN I GET AT YOUR FEET AND GLEAN WISDOM AND SOAK UP SOME OF YOUR ESSENCE?"

In the months to come I pondered that answer and often wondered if it was a copout kind of answer. Was that a fluffy spiritual answer that really meant, "I don't know?" No, it was the truth. You see, when you fall in love with God, you'll look up and realize you're right in the center of His will, which is where your purpose and destiny lie. You do not have to work tirelessly trying to find it on your own. If you take the hand of God, He'll lead you straight to it. Similarly, a mentor will behave the same way. My mentor did not draw me close for her own gain, but she saw that she had been assigned to me to be the gatekeeper of my soul. She poured into me with no expectation of getting anything back for herself but found satisfaction in seeing me grow by leaps and bounds for Christ.

A mentor will not be selfish and want you to herself. She will want what is best for you like Naomi did for her daughter-in-laws. Naomi did not try to keep them for herself despite the fact she was getting old and could use the help. However, she released them to walk in their own destinies. In Ruth 1:8 Naomi says, "Go back to your mothers' home. May the Lord show kindness . . . may the Lord grant each of you husbands."

Nonetheless, Ruth decided to stay with Naomi. Orpah went back to her people, but something compelled Ruth to stay. Unbeknownst to Ruth, it was her destiny that gripped her with such conviction to follow after Naomi, and she said so powerfully: "Entreat me not to leave you or to return from following after you: for wherever you go, I will go and where you lodge, I will lodge, thy people shall be my people, and thy God my God." God has a way of locking us onto our path of destiny even when it is not 100 percent clear to us at that moment. In immediate sight this was

> A MENTORING RELATIONSHIP ORCHESTRATED BY GOD HAS A WAY OF BLESSING BOTH INDIVIDUALS INVOLVED.

a blessing to Naomi, though God had something much bigger in store for Ruth.

A mentoring relationship orchestrated by God has a way of blessing both individuals involved. With the blessing of Ruth remaining by her side, Naomi yet gave her room to grow. Naomi had much reason to be bitter, after losing her husband and both sons, yet in her own loss and pain she did not clip the wings of this young eagle. She had great joy about Ruth meeting Boaz and provided her with wisdom and direction of how to position herself for him. Naomi was genuinely concerned for her well-being and wanted her to be well taken care of. She allowed herself to be used by God to bless Ruth, to steer her into the center of God's will, without becoming covetous or controlling. A healthy mentor will give you advice, but not make decisions for you or try to live her life through you. The relationship may be for a season or a lifetime, but most importantly you are to get what God assigned for her to give to you. Naomi played a key role in Ruth being chosen by Boaz, and they bore Obed, who became David's grandfather through which the lineage of Jesus flows. The Lord used Naomi to bridge Ruth to her future "king"—Boaz—while simultaneously leading her to fulfill the broader purpose of serving as a bridge to *our* King, Jesus Christ!

This is why I say a mentor for life is such a precious covenant and it must be God orchestrated. How devastating would it be to follow after the advice of a mentor all the while leaving the will of God behind to never realize the special purpose for which you were created? That is a scary thought, and that is why we must be careful with who we share our hearts and dreams with.

A godly mentor will always shape you in the way of God, and anything inconsistent of that is worth fleeing from as quickly as possible.

Paul and Timothy are another great example of a mentoring relationship. Paul poured a tremendous amount of wisdom into Timothy, because he saw a special gift in Timothy. Paul reminded him constantly to not neglect his gift, to not let people look down on him, and to guard what was being entrusted to him. He instructed him to hold fast to this wisdom and write it on the tablet of his heart because it would keep him. Paul knew that he would not always be there with Timothy every step of the way, so it was important for Timothy to be able to stand on his own two feet. Sometimes, a mentoring relationship is just for a season, and later the time comes for you to stretch out your wings and fly. A great mentor is not an enabler, but a trainer. An enabler cripples. A trainer empowers and directs growth for greater productivity.

> A TRAINER EMPOWERS AND DIRECTS GROWTH FOR GREATER PRODUCTIVITY.

Paul took Timothy under his wing and gave him sound instruction. He told him the truth about life. He said to Timothy that if he was truly serious about ministry that he would suffer persecution. That is what is so precious about mentors is that they are open to share their struggles and testimonies with you for your benefit that you may avoid the same pitfalls and know what to expect ahead. The most natural mentor is one who has taken a similar path as you. Paul was seasoned in the ministry, and Timothy had just received the call to preach, so he had already walked the path Timothy was starting out on. Paul had the credibility to be able to teach Timothy about the valley lows. Conversely, Timothy had the constant reminder in his mentor, that his dreams were possible. If Paul could do it, so could he.

A great mentor has so many facets, and whatever you need the most, God will amplify in that person. As a young woman entering adulthood, I was seeking how to become a Proverbs 31 woman. I wanted the poise, the elegance, the charm, and the depth. My mentor, in her gentle mothering way, walked with me. She walked with me through life so closely during that season. Coaching me. Praying for me. Comforting me. Praising me. She walked me through the valley lows. She cheered for me when I reached the mountain high. She released me when God had completed the work in my life that He led through her. I don't even think she realized when that season came to an end, but at some point, I no longer needed her hand. Perhaps it was the day when I no longer needed to run to her and tell her every detail of a situation I was facing. Perhaps it was the day, I truly fell in love with that Jesus she had told me so much about. Perhaps it was the day I met my knight in shining armor and he took my hand in holy matrimony. Whatever day it was, that day finally came. I was able to stand on my own two feet. I had become my own woman. The reflection of that Proverbs 31 woman had become so much clearer in me and is coming into better focus with each passing day.

In the Beauty of His Virtue,
Jennifer

Questions to Ponder and Discuss

1. Is there someone in your life that you admire who could serve as a mentor? What qualities does she bear? How does she align with God's Word?

2. Have you had a mentor before? What impact did that person make on your life?

3. Have you considered being a mentor to someone? In what way can you help someone who is younger or less experienced than you?

A *Prayer* TO PRAY

Dear Lord,

Oh, how amazing you are. You are the God of the universe, and yet you know and care about my needs. You separated the water from land and hung the stars in the sky, yet you know me by name. Lord, I thank you for caring for me. I thank you for loving me like I am your only child. I thank you for the little things you do to show me you are there and in control. Always leading me along. Always shaping me in your image.

Lord, I thank you for the mentors you have placed in my life, those who I know personally and those who I admired from a distance. Thank you for their example and your timely placement of them in my path. Please help me to get all that you ordained for them to impart to my life. Thank you for how you have used others to bless me. Help me to do the same for those coming behind me. Help me to realize my potential and make good on every investment that has been made in me in a way that glorifies you. Empower me to be a change agent in the lives of younger women who are where I once was.

In Jesus' Name I pray, Amen.

A friend is one that knows you as you are, understands where you have been, accepts what you have become, and still, gently allows you to grow.

WILLIAM SHAKESPEARE

Letter #6:

LET'S BE GIRLS TOGETHER

My Beloved Sister,

I mentioned in the previous letter the importance of our horizontal relationships, of which mentors are a key component. Additionally, friendships among peers are essential to a robust life as well. It is so important to have girlfriends to do life with, to share the ups and downs, and bursts of laughter! Nonetheless, when you begin walking with God with a renewed fervency, friendships that you had earlier may grow cold and distant. If they are women poor in spirit at worst they are susceptible to betrayal, but more commonly they will shrink back unable to handle the fact that you are blossoming. You must make up in your mind that you are going all the way, that you are going full steam ahead and nothing or nobody will hold you back. Certainly, you don't want to travel this remarkable journey alone, so this is the time to pray for a circle of friends who are heading in your same direction where you can be helpers one to another.

Accountability partners are priceless. Know who your true friends are. They are not just women to run to the mall with. You must know if this is a person or a group of women willing to get down in the trenches with you. Will they be like the friends who pulled the roof off to get their friend to Jesus, or will they walk past you like the priest and the others did to the man lying in the street? Is your deliverance that important to them that they'll tear off the roof of bondage in your life with intercessory prayer to get you to the King? Are you that important to them that they'll carry you when you can't carry yourself? Is your healing and your future that important to them that they'll press through the situation to find an answer even if it is inconvenient and costs them sweat, tears, time, and even money?

Friendships of any sort come with a price, and they come with a level of influence and power you have over each other. Do not let ungodly covenants cause you to miss your destiny. You may say, "I'm strong willed and not easily influenced." Yes, you may not be easily coaxed to do wrong, but are they causing you to go to the next level or are you stuck in your comfort zone because nothing around you is stimulating you to greatness? Friendships should be an investment, not a liability. You should leave from their presence refreshed and empowered, because not only are they fun to dine with or shop with, but they also challenge your thinking, encourage your heart, and inspire you by what is going on in their lives. Your being with them should be a gain. First Corinthians 10:31–32 tells us, "So eat and drink and do everything else for the glory of God. Don't do anything that causes another person to trip and fall. It doesn't matter if that person is a

> **FRIENDSHIPS SHOULD BE AN INVESTMENT NOT A LIABILITY.**

Jew or a Greek or a member of God's church." John 15:13 says, "No one has greater love than the one who gives his life for his friends." Friendships are sacrificial giving and something worth having is worth working for. So the bottom line is this: it will cost you something.

Jesus said in this same chapter, "You are my friends if you do what I command. I do not call you servants anymore. Servants do not know their master's business. Instead, I have called you friends. I have told you everything I learned from my Father." Jesus is saying that I've been intimate with you. I've shared the matters of my heart, and I've revealed myself to you. I've given myself to you, and you know the deep things about me. This is what friendship is about; it is about sharing and growing in knowledge of each other. This is only possible in an atmosphere of trust. Jesus had no reservation because He trusted them. They had walked three years together and had shared some personal struggles together. You cannot share your heart with someone who cannot be trusted. You cannot afford to because it is too costly. Jesus did not stand guard watching to see what they would do with the truth He gave them. He went on to the cross because He knew what was deposited in them was in safekeeping. His confidence was in that He knew His word could not come back void but would accomplish what it was sent to do, and His teaching was for them to establish the kingdom of God in the earth until He returned. When He returns, He is coming back for a glorious church, and it all began with His friends whom He could trust with the very purpose for which He came.

Likewise, with godly covenants you ought not have to call that person every three days to be reassured they are not exposing your secrets. Your heart should rest well with that person and you have confidence that your word will accomplish what it was sent to do. For example, if you shared something that you wanted them to pray for, you should be confident they are lifting you up. If you asked them to check into a job for you, you should know that your resume is in good hands. Nothing given to them will come back void. It won't come back worse or incomplete. You won't have regrets. Proverbs says the wounds of a friend are trusted and the kiss of an enemy is multiplied over. The wounds are trusted because you are sure that their intentions are pure, and their imperfections are innocent. The wound is either something they did mistakenly or in other situations they have given you the truth that hurts.

Beware of friends who have kisses multiplied over. This type can come in different forms. She may be one to always make up with gifts or seem to be really into you, but there really is no depth and everything is superficial. Perhaps she is the one with the trail of mess behind her and is always coming to you pleading her innocence and playing the victim role. Or maybe she's the one who lifts you up in your presence and bashes other women in their absence. She likes you but doesn't like herself. This is a dangerous woman. She's covetous of you. She is cunning and manipulative for her own gain, but so blinded by her own pain. She is your classic "fake it till you make it" and is in desperate need of help. It is her mask that makes her functional in public. You must flee her emotionally and break covenant. Show her the love of God but remove yourself from this unhealthy relationship.

We have a biblical example of what a beautiful friendship looks like in 1 Samuel chapters 18–20. David and Jonathan are the epitome of such a covenant. Jonathan's father, Saul, became jealous of David because the Spirit of the Lord and His favor were upon David and had left him. Saul's jealousy brewed to the point of hatred, and eventually he wanted to kill David. With this news, David began to flee for his life. In this story we see the purity of Jonathan's heart because he didn't just stand with his dad simply because that was his dad, but he stood for righteousness. The truth was that David was innocent, and the purity of Jonathan's heart wanted to see justice prevail.

This was a crisis for David, and in his panic, he asks Jonathan, "What have I done that your father wants me killed?"[38] Jonathan responds by speaking life to him: "No, you are not going to die and in fact whatever you want me to do I will do for you."[39] You see, a true friend is not going to see you in a crisis and leave you there. Jonathan created a plan for his safety and then went to his dad's banquet to see if these accusations and plots were true. Saul inquired about David after two days of being absent from the feast and Jonathan told him he went to join his family in a sacrifice. Saul's anger flared up, and he hurled his spear at Jonathan. It was at that point he knew that his dad's intentions were ill towards David. Jonathan grieved at his father's shameful act towards David and he was determined to get down in the trenches with David. He simply could not forsake him now. It was either all or nothing, and Jonathan chose to stand in the gap for him. David had said that there was only a step between him and death, and Jonathan took it upon himself to stand right there between David and death. Why would he do this? It seems so risky and costly, right? Well, Jonathan did it because he loved David as he loved himself. What a powerful and selfless love. It was his act out of love for David that spared David's life. Jonathan gave him directions to flee, and in their last meeting Jonathan said, "Go in peace. In the name of the Lord we have taken an oath. We've promised to be friends. We've said, 'The Lord is a witness between you and me. He's a witness between your children and my children forever.'"[40] Now that's a serious godly covenant! That is what God desires of us. The Lord says love your neighbor as yourself because love is the fulfillment of the law. It we can get love right we don't need to hear repeatedly, "Do not steal, do not kill, do not covet your neighbors possessions." If we can love with an all-encompassing, unconditional agape love, love will produce victory over the enemy every time. This is the model of friendship we must model ourselves after. This is the kind of covenant that helps us prosper and move in our purpose because it brings out the best in everyone. David was a young man when this happened, and do you realize that if Jonathan did not do what he did that David could have died and have never become king? He would not have fulfilled the purpose for which God created him. Most importantly, if Saul had killed him from what lineage would our Savior Jesus had come?

In contrast, I want to share with you a biblical story of an ungodly covenant. I mentioned earlier that friendship warrants a certain measure of power you have over each other. In case you didn't believe me, I'd like to argue my case. There is a story in the Bible about a man name Amnon. Amnon fell in love with his sister Tamar, and he wanted to have her sexually. This was an internal struggle and something sinful that he needed to resolve. Nonetheless, he decides to tell a friend. Second Samuel 13:3 tells us that Amnon had a friend named Jonadab who was very shrewd. He shared this lustful desire with him, and instead of Jonadab saying, "No, do not do this awful thing to your sister," he tells Amnon *how* to rape her! Do you see the influence friends can have? David had a dilemma, and Jonathan showed him how to save his life. In this story, Amnon revealed a weakness to an even weaker vessel that cost him his life. Tamar's brother Absalom ultimately killed Amnon for raping her. Was Amnon's purpose fulfilled in the earth realm, or was the sin in his heart, which Jonadab preyed upon, the short circuit to his demise? We'll never know but one thing we do know is that you pay a price to be friends. So, ask yourself, what price am I willing to pay?

IT IS AMAZING WHAT HAPPENS WHEN WE ACTUALLY WAIT ON GOD.

My accountability circle has been one of my greatest life investments. Certainly, this achievement did not come without trial and error. After a major upset and feeling betrayed, I knew it was time for a new set of friends. What I did differently in that time of transition was pray that the Lord would send me friends *He* wanted me to have, friends for life, friends who could be trusted, friends who loved the Lord. It is amazing what happens when we actually wait on God. The friends I have now are the answers to that prayer I prayed, and the Lord sent confirmation after confirmation that these were relationships He was orchestrating.

When God gives you a harvest, it is sweet and perfect for you. The Word says, "The blessings of the Lord add no sorrow," and friendships are such a blessing. Godly friends are a breath of fresh air, and I have enjoyed doing life with my sister girls. We are women who are on fire for God, walking in greatness and authority. We are a source of encouragement to each other, a ball of laughter, and a shoulder to lean on when the going gets tough.

A vital thing I must mention is that in no way is an accountability circle synonymous to a clique. There is not one personality, one voice, or one clothing style the group succumbs to. It is a friendship circle where everyone is free to be themselves and are encouraged to be the best woman God is calling each one to be and have fun doing it! For me, these are the friends who helped me through some tough times, just as I have helped them. Any time one of us has struggled, whether it is love life or work life, we are there for each other. We have prayed and cried and prayed and talked and cried some more and prayed some more. Whatever it took, we never gave up on each other.

I remember the phase I went through right before I met my husband. My love life seemed turbulent. I had this clear promise from the Lord that I would get married in that season of my life, but surely God did not show me the process of what it would take to get there! Nor did he show me Mr. Right either! Only after an intense heartbreak, did I finally learn to let God write my love story. It was just as Eric and Leslie Ludy writes in their book, *When God Writes Your Love Story:* "My God-written love story began at that moment. God took the pen from my trembling hand and began scripting the most incredible tale imaginable. No, my future husband did not show up at my front door right then. But from that day on, God began healing and restoring the pain of my mistakes and molding and preparing me for true love."

My friends were there through it all. Never judged. Always loved. Always spoke God's Word and always prayed for God's best for me. They helped me get up and put the pieces of my heart together. They helped ready me for my king. And when my wedding day came, I was able to walk down the aisle a pure bride with total confidence in my heart that I was marrying the man God had for me. I was no longer blurred or sabotaged by the enemy's counterfeiting ways, but it was a love that God put between my king and me. It was a destiny decision, divine intervention, and the reward of total submission of me to my Lord.

Your Covenant Sister,
Jennifer

Questions TO PONDER AND DISCUSS

1. What friends do you have that you are sure God sent? What gives you that certainty?

2. Are there friendships that need reevaluating? How can you remove yourself from these relationships and position yourself for godly covenants?

3. What kind of friend are you? Are you the friend you desire to have? If not, how can you improve?

A *Prayer* TO PRAY

Dear heavenly Father,

You are the greatest friend ever, and I am so glad you call me friend. I thank you for your love that reaches so far, so deep, so wide. Your love washes over my sin and sees me in the beauty of your holiness. Thank you for walking with me. Come rain or come sunshine, you are always there, and I thank you.

I thank you for the friends you have given me and those you are preparing to send into my life. Help us to be accountable to each other and cause each other to grow and maximize our potential in every area of life. No jealousy shall reign in our hearts. Our love shall be pure for each other as the friendship love David and Jonathan shared. Help us love each other when one seems unlovable. Help us speak the truth, even if it hurts. Help us stand in the gap and pray each other through when life crumbles and directions are few. Help us celebrate each other and help each other succeed. Let your love be our standard. Let your presence permeate our covenant. Let your Spirit bind us together as friends for life.

In Jesus' Name, Amen.

The ultimate measure of a man is not where he stands in moments of comfort and convenience, but where he stands at times of challenge and controversy.

MARTIN LUTHER KING, JR.

Letter #7:

READIED FOR MY KING

My Beloved Sister,

I hope you have enjoyed our discussion of horizontal relationships. We can truly enjoy these relationships once we've taken the time to get the vertical one right with our Lord and Savior Jesus Christ. Our horizontal relationships of mentors and girlfriends are priceless. They are a source of leadership, encouragement, and fun! But there is another component of horizontal relationships that is so very precious, the most work, and the most gratifying when it is God-ordained, and that is the marital relationship. Deciding who you spend the rest of your earthly life with is one of the most important decisions you will make next to where you will spend eternity. It is such a huge decision that you cannot afford to get it wrong.

There are so many things that we can discuss regarding having a successful marriage: from finances to communication, to sex, to raising children, and work-life balance. The list is endless, and there are plenty of books on the market that cover such topics. However, what I feel impressed upon my heart to share with you in this letter is the idea of submission. Many people hate the word "submission"; somehow, it has been dirtied and misunderstood as bondage and oppression, which is the furthest thing from the truth. This is the reason why I'd like to explore it a bit further.

The first thing that is required of us as Christians is submission to God. True submission to the Father is a life of freedom. When we are truly living for the Lord, we are free from the hold of the enemy. We are free in our minds and empowered to create, produce, and think outside the box. Most importantly, we are free to worship, free to enter God's presence, see His face, and not turn away in shame.

> TRUE SUBMISSION TO THE FATHER IS A LIFE OF FREEDOM.

This is what true submission brings when we submit to our heavenly King. The ironic thing is that it is not much different when you put that in the context of submission to our husbands.

The Lord has already given us His take on submission in marriage in His Word. He says for wives to submit to your husbands.[42] The husband is the head as Christ is the head of the church.[43] To be clear, it does not say husbands are the dictator or husbands can walk all over their wives. It says husbands are the head as Christ is the head, and what did Christ do for his bride? He laid down his life! So, if this is the framework for marriage and Christ is the standard, the most fundamental questions to ask yourself concerning a relationship are as follows: Is this the man God would have me to be submitted to, and is he a godly man who would lay down his life for his family?

For my single sisters, if the answer is no, you can more easily walk away because there is no marriage covenant yet, especially if there are no children. But even if there are children involved, that does not mean you have to stay and be miserable. You do not have to marry a person simply because a child was born out of the relationship if the relationship is not glorifying to God. Do not keep digging. Just because life got off course doesn't mean you keep going in that direction. There is forgiveness, and God will welcome you back. If there is life in your body, there is still time for change and growth. It is never too late. Certainly, premarital sex is sin, but the child is not a mistake. God is the *only* giver of life, and for every life He creates, He has a plan and purpose. Nonetheless, the relationship with the father of the child may not be God's plan for your life. The last thing you want is to be unequally yoked and outside of God's will. It is too costly. God has more in store for you, and you are worth more than what you are settling for. If the relationship is broken and unhealthy, you must get out. Your life depends on it. Everything you were created for is at stake.

> GOD IS THE *ONLY* GIVER OF LIFE, AND FOR EVERY LIFE HE CREATES, HE HAS A PLAN AND PURPOSE.

For my married sisters, if the answer is no to the question, then things must truly be bad. There is something structurally unsound and the foundation is broken. There may be some form of abuse, infidelity, or merely one or both of you were not mature at the time of marrying and now there are severe incompatibilities.

Whether it is something I named or something else, if you truly think this is not the man God would have you submit to, then it is a marriage that is not what it should be in God's eyes.

Walking away is costly. Divorce hurts; divorce is sin. It is messy, and there are always repercussions. However, if you truly know in your heart of hearts that you messed up with this decision and no amount of prayer or counseling can make it what it should be, then you cannot allow this relationship to become your death sentence. This might sound controversial to some, and I am in no way advocating for divorce, but if you married out of disobedience and disobedience is what separates us from God, then I do not believe it is God's will to remain in that darkness, separated from Him. There is forgiveness, and it may be worth going through the consequences of undoing what got you to this place to finally get on the right track, in covenant with God, and ready to live an abundant, healthy life.

Surely, this is a decision that needs much prayer and godly counsel for God's direction, because sometimes there is a real hope for the situation and you may need clarity to see that. There are plenty of stories of marriages that have triumphed over drug addiction, infidelity, abuse, selfishness, immaturity, or whatever the struggle may be, and that can very well be your testimony. Sometimes the person may have been right for you, but the timing was wrong, which made things more tumultuous than it should have been. Or possibly it could be that the enemy is simply trying to destroy what God put together in His perfect timing, and the disillusionment of the hardship is causing you to think the right answer is to give up and throw in the towel.

This is such a delicate situation and sensitive time for you that it is imperative to seek the Lord regarding your circumstances. The key thing is that if you cannot say with a resounding yes this is the man God would have me submit to, then something is critically wrong and must be addressed ASAP. Living in such distress and limbo does not position you to walk in power and be effective to fulfill your purpose. So please, I implore you today to take action and fix it so that we can rise up together as mighty women in God, ready to crush Satan's head and do great things for God's kingdom.

> HE HAS VISION, BUT HE LEADS FIRST BY EXAMPLE AND THEN WITH A GENTLE HAND.

For you ladies who answered yes, I rejoice with you because it is a beautiful thing and so very important. It is the foundation to everything, and it is worth waiting for and praying for. A man who is worthy of your submission is a man after God's own heart. He loved the Lord first before he loved you. He is a man's man! He carries himself well, with respect and dignity. He knows who he is and where he is going. He respects you as the jewel you are, the daughter of the most high King, and he does not abuse his authority like a tyrant or dictator. He has vision, but he leads first by example and then with a gentle hand. He is strong in character and productivity, but not aggressive in nature. He knows sacrifice and he knows hard work; he meets both with square shoulders and planted feet. He is your lord, your king.

To be ready for such a man, you must be ready to

serve him and serve the children of this beautiful union. It means to be ready to be in a lifetime partnership, sink or swim. Whether the business fails or prospers. Whether the waistline expands or stays the same. It is a partnership that stands the test of time and the test of life's curveballs. Lastly, it means to be ready to choose to love even

NEVER LET THE 20 PERCENT BE YOUR 100 PERCENT FOCUS, BUT LET THE 80 PERCENT BE YOUR 100 PERCENT FOCUS.

in the moments when he seems unlovable. Yes, he's your knight in shining armor and your superman, but he is also human. He will have bad days. He may say the wrong thing from time to time or forget the very thing you asked him to remember. He may even have stinky socks and bad breath in the morning. Yes, indeed. Nevertheless, you must remember that this is the 20 percent. The 80 percent is everything I told you he was in the preceding paragraph, and that is why you married him or why you're praying until he comes. The 80 percent is who you praise and highly esteem. The 20 percent is who you are sensitive towards, understanding, and forgiving. Never let the 20 percent be your 100 percent focus, but let the 80 percent be your 100 percent focus. The enemy would like for you to dwell on the 20 percent to sow seeds of discord and distract you from the blessing you have. The minor imperfections are a part of life, and the grass is never greener on the other side. It's only green where you have watered and fertilized. So, invest in your relationship, laying everything on the line, holding back nothing, and get ready to embrace what God can do in and through your union.

THE READYING PROCESS

For those of you reading this who aren't already married but would like to get married one day, I would like to emphasize it is very important to be ready. To ensure a secure foundation and bright future for your marriage, take your preparation seriously. You must be like Esther in readying yourself for your king. It's not something that happens overnight; it's a transformation from the inside out over a selected period God authorizes. It may be six months for one woman or six years for another. The bottom line is that you want the man God has for you and nothing less. Thus, you must be willing to wait on His timing, and your spiritual health is key to making this successful. Knowing your God in an intimate way prepares you to minister to your husband and be a prudent wife. Walking with God wholeheartedly teaches you selflessness, the depth of intimacy, real love, forgiveness, and how to be purpose driven and destiny minded, yet with the ability to be submitted to your husband and his vision. These qualities come by prayer, reading the Word, worship, consecration, and fellowship with other Spirit-filled Christians.

DEVELOPING A PRAYER LIFE

Developing a prayer life is vital to your spiritual growth. It is your time to be with God and share the matters of your heart. Prayer is our communion with God. We can place our worries, fears, and situations at the foot of the cross. The Word says, "Cast all your anxiety upon him because he cares for you."[44] God sees and knows all things, but prayer is our avenue to invite God into the private matters of our lives. He wants you to entreat Him.

He wants to know you want Him. He said, "I'll draw nigh if you draw nigh to me." The purpose of prayer is to speak your heart, have God speak to your heart, and then allow him to transform your heart.

Entering worship is a deeper level of intimacy that entreats the Father. With a worship experience, it cannot be a "hi and bye" prayer—you must press in. You need to quiet yourself, turn off the television—some quiet worship music is fine—and enter into His presence. Don't just run your mouth, but share your heart, and don't be so quick to get up. Stay there. Let the Lord know you're serious and hungry for Him. Draw Him by worship. Tell him how wonderful He is and how much He means to you. Tell him how He's exalted and holy. Worship Him for who He is. He is a majestic God. God and God alone. Tell him these things. Bless his Holy Name.

When you speak your heart to God, it is a way to open yourself up to Him. Tell him your pain, desires, issues—whatever. God has broad shoulders; whatever the situation is, He can carry it. Relieve yourself of the burden of carrying everything, and take the things you can't change on your own to Him. Vent to Him, cry on His shoulder, don't nag others but share the irritation and anxiousness with God. Make your requests known, repent, pray the Word of God, and declare the promises of God. This is what we do in speaking our hearts to God. There is no prescribed method. It is simply being yourself in the face of the One who made you. It doesn't matter if your makeup runs or if your words don't come out right. He is our Father who loves us regardless. He is our Creator who wove us together in our mothers' wombs.

Now when you've gotten everything out on the table

and you've said everything you could possibly say, however many times you felt you needed to say it, stay there. Don't run off. Don't sign off so soon. Let Him speak to your heart. Let the God of the universe penetrate the depths of your soul. Let His arms wrap you in His everlasting love. Let Him breathe fresh life into you. Let Him be your Daddy and tell you He's got everything under control and you can rest in His care. Let Him give you direction if that is what is needed in that hour. Let Him reprimand and convict as needed. Let Him pour in wisdom or simply affirm His love. No prayer time will be the same. Seasons change. Your needs change. But the great thing about it is that we serve a God who stays the same, and His ultimate objective never changes: that we reflect Him more and bring Him glory.

Growing in our intimacy with God is a twofold process. We first come to know Him better, and then He transforms our hearts. He will cause you to think differently, become more like Him in character, and change your desires to His.

GETTING INTO GOD'S WORD

Furthermore, you should make it a point to get into the Word daily. Feed your spirit just as you feed your natural man. Pray before you begin reading and ask that He'll direct you and that He will speak to you from the riches of His Word and bring illumination, understanding, and revelation. Pray that He will give you a *rhema* word, a word for the now. Don't read the Bible like it is a history book or a novel, but treat it like it is holy, sacred, and the God-breathed living Word that it is. Have some focus to your study, so that you are not overwhelmed. Chew off of small pieces and pour over those Scriptures to really digest the meaning. Get a version of the Bible you understand and credible supplemental materials like a concordance, Bible dictionary, study guide, or devotional.

First Peter chapter 3 says, "Your beauty should not come from outward adornment, such as braided hair and the wearing of gold jewelry and fine clothes. Instead, it should be that of your inner self, the unfading beauty of a gentle and quiet spirit, which is of great worth in God's sight. For this is the way the holy women of the past who put their hope in God used to make themselves beautiful."

This is what makes you beautiful. This is what draws a true man of God. This is what separates you from the worldly women. Your beauty is lasting, and it shines from within. It has depth and is pleasing to God. When you're beautiful because of the presence of God in your life and the sweetness of His Spirit within you, you won't have to strategically position yourself to be seen by men. Proverbs 31 says, "A wife of noble character who can find? Her worth is far above rubies." This speaks to who is the man who has the eyes to see her? God conceals a woman of this magnitude. A man of the world is not drawn to this. But a man after God's own heart will notice you even if you did not notice him. Something will leap in him and say, "Bone of my bone and flesh of my flesh."

When we talk about being ready for our king, three powerful women of the Bible come to mind: Rebekah, Esther, and Ruth. What I love about these three women is that they were focused and content with where they were in life. You do not see their lives as the story of women who chased after the man of their dreams. You see three women, submitted to a God they trusted to make dreams happen. Each woman was set about doing her day's work when destiny knocked. And when destiny knocked, they were ready to answer. This supernatural intersection of your life with God's choice man for you is not something you scout after. It is not as if you hang your head out the window of life looking up and down the street wondering what's taking so long. When you do such things, you invite the wrong company. The right man comes when you are industrious, set about your work vigorously, and content with who you are and where you are.

ESTHER

What God has given to you and endowed you with is not for your pleasure and indulgence alone. Esther was a small-town Jewish girl, elevated to queen of Persia as a mark of destiny. It reminds us that to whom much is given, much is required; and, for such a time as this, it was divine alignment that she could intervene on behalf of a generation. What's amazing about Esther is that she was a submitted woman, to her Lord and her husband. When Mordecai came to her about going before the king on behalf of the Jews to save them from the death sentence Haman contrived, Mordecai said, "Do not think because you are in the King's house you alone of all the Jews will escape. For if you remain silent at this time, relief and deliverance for the Jews will arise from another place, but you and your father's family will perish. And who knows but that you have come to royal position for such a time as this?"[45]

What powerful words! Esther's heart was attuned to the Spirit of God, and immediately before deciding she went into prayer. She called a fast and gathered those around her to do the same. She decided to go before the king, knowing the consequences of breaking tradition that she could be killed for going before the king without being summoned. But knowing what was at stake for her people, she said, "If I perish, I perish." What a brave and noble woman!

We have to be sold out just the same way, but not in a reckless fashion. With prayer and supplication, the Spirit will lead us individually as to what we are called to do, but we have to be attuned to what God is saying or else we can miss it. Just as Mordecai said to Esther, "The Jews will be delivered regardless of whether you help, but this may be the opportunity for God to use you!" This may be what God has fashioned together for your life, and are you willing to lay everything on the line to be a part of it? Such a sobering ultimatum, and what is amazing about God is that He wants us to step out onto the water, step out of our comfort zones and our own might, and embrace and experience the infinite power of Him. We cannot be all God has called us to be or partake of all what God has for us by staying in the boat. Faith is the substance of things hoped for and the evidence of things unseen.[46] If you can see it, it isn't faith; that's called your comfort zone!

REBEKAH

Then there is Rebekah. Not much is ever said about her, besides the fact that she was Isaac's wife and seemed to play a part in Jacob "deceiving" his father for the blessing. Interestingly, what ultimately happened with Jacob and Esau had already been told to her when the boys were yet in the womb.

Nonetheless, what is remarkable about Rebekah, something we can glean from her life, is that she was industrious. When destiny knocked in her life, she was busy at work. She was minding her business drawing water for the day when the servant of Abraham approached her. When he requested water from her, she did not hesitate. She even went above and beyond to provide water for his camels, which was not a light task. He had ten thirsty camels, and Rebekah drew water for them all until they had their fill. She was not lazy; she did not complain and did not stop until the task was completed. She not only was beautiful for the eye to behold, but she had endurance, a servant's heart, and a zest about her that was captivating.

When the servant saw that his prayers had been answered and Rebekah was the one he had come for to take back as Isaac's bride, there was not only the servant's confirmation she was the right pick, but also her family confirmed it. There is something very valuable and godly about a family's affirmation of a relationship, and it serves every young maid well. Any relationship that causes family turmoil needs to be reassessed, especially when you have godly parents who hear from the Lord.

RUTH

My favorite story of all is in the book of Ruth. Ruth stuck close to wisdom and was faithful. She left all to follow God when she chose to follow Naomi. What is amazing about such sacrifice is that it is not about God *requiring* all, but what happens to a person when they are *willing* to give all. The reward is breathtaking, and we see the results as we explore the life of Ruth. She was focused, hardworking, selfless, and humble. Ruth 2:10 says, "She bowed with her face to the ground." She was modest and a giver as she brought food back to Naomi on a regular basis. She was obedient and listened to wisdom. Then, most importantly, she was settled and focused on her work. She was diligent and not anxious for anything, and it is at this time God began strategically positioning her unbeknownst to her as she worked in Boaz's field.[47]

What is so important about this is that in the right timing your Boaz will take notice of you and find you. God's Word says, "He who findeth a wife findeth a good thing and obtaineth favour from the Lord."[48] It doesn't say, "She who causes herself to be seen is found and this is a good thing." As women of God, we must let the men be the seekers, just as Boaz did thousands of years ago, and it still works today. There at a distance he inquired of Ruth, "Whose damsel is that?" If your Boaz inquired of you today, what report would he receive? The men that worked alongside spoke of her diligence and hard work.[49] She was working, taking care of her home, and not looking for handouts. She was busy with her work and not desperately looking for a husband. It is at a time when you are settled caring for the things of the Lord your Boaz will come for you. And when he comes, he is ready to make provisions for you. In verses 8 through 9 of chapter 2, Boaz told Ruth to not glean another field; he gave her shelter and became her covering by telling the men to not touch her. He gave her food and direction. He took notice of her sacrifice and was drawn to her inner woman. He was respectful and gentle as Ruth responds to him by saying, "May I continue to find favor in your eyes, my lord. You have given me comfort and have spoken kindly to your servant."[50]

WHEN YOUR TRUE BOAZ SHOWS UP, HE SHOULD MAKE YOUR LIFE EASIER.

When your true Boaz shows up, he should make your life easier. He should not bring chaos and destruction, but his shoulders should be broad enough to build a family on. He should enhance your life and bless you. Ruth 2:14 says, "Ruth had more than enough and when she went to glean, Boaz sent orders ahead of her that the men leave grain out for her to gather and not to embarrass her but to help her." Boaz will send you back full and Ruth had eaten enough and yet had much to carry back and share. Her mother-in-law took notice of how much she had gathered, and people around you will see how well kept you are as a wife. A wife should blossom in the care of her Boaz. She ought not be worn down, frail, and empty, but her countenance and spirit should be full, and life-giving. Then finally, what is so attractive about Boaz is that he is respectful and pursues Ruth by going through the appropriate chains of command for her release. He went to the elders and kinsman of the town. A real godly man will not overstep authority and disrespect those who are over you, whether it is your parents, pastor, or God Himself. Boaz knows the proper way to secure his bride is by going to the number one source—God. If God approves, then the natural authority will confirm it and release you accordingly.

Praying for your True Boaz,
Jennifer

Questions TO PONDER AND DISCUSS

1. What are some things in your life right now that you can focus on until your Boaz comes?

2. How can you prepare for his arrival, but not be anxious?

3. Do you have any fears concerning getting married?

4. For those who are married, how did you spend your single life? Do you have any regrets?

5. For those who are married, now you that are married, what do you wish you had known prior to getting married?

A *Prayer* TO PRAY

Dear heavenly Father,

You are my true love, and I give you all of me. Lord, I am totally committed to you, and my heart cares for the things of you. Free me of the anxiety of not knowing when will my Boaz come, and help me to trust you that he is en route. Lord, please write my love story. I do not want to mar the beauty of your manuscript for my life. I want a love that brings you glory and a love that will stand the test of time and the struggles of this life. Lord, please help me to be industrious like Ruth, submissive like Rebekah, and Spirit filled like Esther. Lord, I need you to calm the longings of my heart and cover it with your blood so that I will not be led astray or settle for less than your very best. And lastly, Lord, when the time comes that I am inquired of, let it be said of me that I am a daughter of the most high King, a woman of great character, strong work ethic, and inner strength.

In Jesus' Name I pray, Amen.

It is, perhaps, one of the hardest struggles
of the Christian life to learn this sentence:
"Not unto us, not unto us, but unto Thy name be glory."

CHARLES SPURGEON

Letter #8:

REFRESHED FOR A
NEW BEGINNING

My Beloved Sister,

I have written you eight letters, and ironically so, the number eight is the biblical number meaning "new beginning." It is my prayer that these letters written from my heart and birthed through my own struggles and triumphs will mark a new beginning in your life as it has done for mine. I wanted this to be written in a straightforward, honest, and concise manner to lay bare to you the most difficult challenges women may face that can hinder us from having a successful life. Then I wanted to give you some clear direction as to how to overcome these barriers. Living a sold-out life for Christ in this twenty-first century can seem nearly impossible, but I wanted this to be a reminder to you that God is yet on the throne and is using His sons and daughters to establish His kingdom.

Living a life as a Proverbs 31 woman can seem like some kind of fantasy as we see discouraging divorce rates. Therefore, we must go back to the basics of holy living that are timeless and work beautifully. If we truly

WE MUST GO BACK TO THE BASICS OF HOLY LIVING THAT ARE TIMELESS AND WORK BEAUTIFULLY.

want to be the woman and wife God is expecting us to be, we just cannot do it the way the world does it. God has provided us a handbook for His prescribed lifestyle of what the family should be, and I wanted to bring illumination to these biblical truths and remind us that they work.

Women of God, let us not fix our eyes on the iconic successful women of the world, but on what God deems as acceptable and beautiful. The hard truth that we must swallow as Christian women desiring to be godly wives is that anything that would cause us to shirk our responsibilities as wives must be reevaluated. God would not place a calling on your life that would cause you to be unavailable to minister to your husband's needs. Your first calling is to your husband, your head, and then to your children. This is your ministry. This is God's order. This is our reference point for doing anything else because all else is secondary. This does not mean that this is all you can do. I, too, have a fire in my belly to do great things just as you do. But we must be in order and submitted to our husbands, as this is pleasing to our Lord.[51] We cannot run off with that fire because we are "so talented and passionate," nor should our husbands try to snuff it out. But, as women of wisdom, we must have it subjected to the will of God and be willing to help our husbands birth the vision God gave him for our lives. The late Dr. Myles Monroe said it best in his book *Understanding the Purpose and Power of Woman*: "As a woman, even though you may be talented, educated, intellectual, experienced, eloquent, and well-dressed, God says, 'I gave you all of these things, not only for your own enrichment and enjoyment, but so that you can be a help to men. You need to use these gifts in your position of helper, of co-leader.'"[52]

Let us not use the fire to burn up our homes, but let it be the light for all to see a godly family reflecting His image. When you do this, there will be peace in your home and a love between you and your husband that is so rich and pure, only an intimacy that God Himself could have created. When you get in position alongside your husband, the two of you will birth the next level out of each other, and this is glorifying to God! Sometimes you just have to push through the fundamentals, and I promise you, Sister, that if you help your husband to birth his dreams and visions, he will soon be in a position to help you birth yours! Proverbs 31:10–31 says the following:

> A wife of noble character who can find?
>   She is worth far more than rubies.
> Her husband has full confidence in her
>   and lacks nothing of value.
> She brings him good, not harm,
>   all the days of her life.
> She selects wool and flax
>   and works with eager hands.
> She is like the merchant ships,
>   bringing her food from afar.
> She gets up while it is still night;
>   she provides food for her family
>   and portions for her female servants.

She considers a field and buys it;
    out of her earnings she plants a vineyard.
She sets about her work vigorously;
    her arms are strong for her tasks.
She sees that her trading is profitable,
    and her lamp does not go out at night.
In her hand she holds the distaff
    and grasps the spindle with her fingers.
She opens her arms to the poor
  and extends her hands to the needy.
When it snows, she has no fear for her household;
    for all of them are clothed in scarlet.
She makes coverings for her bed;
    she is clothed in fine linen and purple.
Her husband is respected at the city gate,
    where he takes his seat among the elders of the land.
She makes linen garments and sells them,
    and supplies the merchants with sashes.
She is clothed with strength and dignity;
    she can laugh at the days to come.
She speaks with wisdom,
    and faithful instruction is on her tongue.
She watches over the affairs of her household
    and does not eat the bread of idleness.
Her children arise and call her blessed;
    her husband also, and he praises her:
"Many women do noble things,
    but you surpass them all."
Charm is deceptive, and beauty is fleeting;
    but a woman who fears the LORD is to be praised.
Honor her for all that her hands have done,
    and let her works bring her praise at the city gate.[53]

IT MEANS WE
PLAY A PART
IN CARRYING
OUT THE
VISION OUR
HUSBANDS
HAVE.

I would like to highlight that verse 11 says, "Her husband has full confidence in her and lacks nothing of value." Verse 23 says, "Her husband is respected at the city gate, where he takes his seat among the elders of the land." During biblical times, the city gate was where business was con-ducted and where the leaders of the community sat. So, this first conveys that a Proverbs 31 kind of woman is married to a leader.

Additionally, verse 31 says, "To honor her for all that her hands have done, and let her works bring her praise at the city gate." Do you remember who is at the city gate? Her husband is at the city gate! My Sisters, that means our work is meaningful. It means we play a part in carrying out the vision our husbands have. He is charged with the leadership, but he is not expected to do it alone. Proverbs 12:4 says, "A wife of noble character is her husband's crown, but a disgraceful wife is like decay in his bones." Women of God, let us be the crown jewel for our husbands and not the Jezebel that defiles and destroys. Moreover, the Word says houses and wealth are inherited from parents, but a prudent wife is from the LORD.[54] This means we are literally a gift from God! We can't be inherited or bought. God has fashioned such an amazing thing!

The last thought I will leave you with is a question regarding the decision you have to make of how you are going to live this life here on earth. Do you want bangles or B.A.N.G.L.E.S.? This is your ultimatum, and it will be a decision before you daily. Bangles are a kind of jewelry worn on the wrists that are technically several layers of bracelets. Bangles are used to self-adorn and make oneself beautiful. B.A.N.G.L.E.S. stands for **B**eauty **A**ll **N**atural, **G**lorifying the **L**ord with **E**verything, **S**tripped. What I mean by *Beauty All Natural* is beauty that is more than skin deep or makeup deep. It is an authentic beauty from being physically, emotionally, and spiritually healthy as a woman. This is about positioning ourselves internally for God's will. *Glorifying the Lord with Everything* is about our external positioning. It is the determination and intentional life to make our friendships, marriage, finances, and everything we are connected to glorifying to God. Lastly, *Stripped* is about transparency, laying down our lives, our wants, our desires, and taking up this life in Christ. It is not about "me" anymore. It is no longer about what can God do for me, but what can I do for God. We are the hands and feet of Jesus to minister to this world.

First Peter 3:3–6 says, "Your beauty should not come from outward adornment, such as elaborate hairstyles and the wearing of gold jewelry or fine clothes. Rather, it should be that of your inner self, the unfading beauty of a gentle and quiet spirit, which is of great worth in God's sight. For this is the way the holy women of the past who put their hope in God used to adorn themselves. They submitted themselves to their own husbands, like Sarah, who obeyed Abraham and called him her lord. You are her daughters if you do what is right and do not give way to fear."

So, I ask again, do you want bangles or B.A.N.G.L.E.S.?

Do you want the temporary pleasures of this world or do you want all that God has for you that lasts for all of eternity? This is your decision and only you can make it. It is my prayer that you join me and so many other sisters around the world who have fixed their stilettos on the path of Jesus, holding back nothing, ready to build God's kingdom, and experience His glory like never before.

Living for Eternity,
Jennifer

Questions TO PONDER AND DISCUSS

1. What excites you about the Proverbs 31 woman?

2. What overwhelms you about the Proverbs 31 woman?

3. What messaging are you getting from the world, social media, and Hollywood of how to be as a woman?

4. What is beautiful to God?

5. How have you struggled or succeeded at living out Proverbs 31 virtues?

A *Prayer* TO PRAY

Dear Lord,

I repent of my sins. I repent of not putting you first. I repent of being too busy for your Word and your presence. Lord, I repent of my selfishness and shortsightedness in not looking beyond my own wants and comforts. But Lord, on this day I commit my life into your hands, to be a tool in your kingdom and a vessel for your use. Put your words in my mouth and fill me with your Spirit, O Lord. Let my heart beat after righteousness and long for the things that are dear to your heart. Help me yield my life, my resources, and time to you so that moment by moment I am in line with your will for my life and never miss an opportunity to bring you glory, whether it is a simple act of obedience or a sacrifice to make a difference. Let my thoughts be heavenward, my actions kingdom minded, and my heart ready to humbly serve. Lastly, Lord, please place your anointing on my life that I may be effective in everything that I do, that I live a life of maximum impact, so that on that day you call me home and I see you face-to-face, you can say, "Well done, my good and faithful servant. You did everything I created you to do," It's no longer about me, Lord . . . my story for *your* glory.[55]

In Jesus' Name I pray, Amen.

Notes

Preface

1. Rom. 7:18b–19 NIV.

Introduction

2. Job 14:1.

3. John 10:10,14:16–18, 26.

4. Isa. 41:10–13, 2 Cor. 10:4.

5. Prov. 31:10.

Letter #1

6. Anne Graham Lotz, *My Heart's Cry* (Tennessee: W Publishing Group, 2002), 43.

Letter #2

7. "Sexual Risk Behaviors: HIV, STD, and Teen Pregnancy Prevention," Centers for Disease Control and Prevention, accessed October 3, 2017, https://www.cdc.gov/healthyyouth/sexualbehaviors/.

8. "National Survey of Family Growth," CDC- Centers for Disease Control and Prevention, published June 22, 2017, https://www.cdc.gov/nchs/nsfg/key_statistics/n.htm#numberlifetime.

9. M.C. Black, K.C. Basile, M.J. Breiding, S.G. Smith, M.L. Walters, M.T. Merrick, J. Chen, and M.R. Stevens, *The National Intimate Partner and Sexual Violence Survey*

(NISVS): 2010 Summary Report (Atlanta, GA: National Center for Injury Prevention and Control, Centers for Disease Control and Prevention, 20111), http://www.cdc.gov/ViolencePrevention/pdf/NISVS_Report2010-a.pdf.

10. Callie Marie Rennison, *Rape and sexual assault: Reporting to police and medical attention, 1992–2000,* (NCJ 194530, U.S. Department of Justice, Office of Justice Programs, Bureau of Justice Statistics, 2002), http://bjs.ojp.usdoj.gov/content/pub/pdf/rsarp00.pdf.

11. T.R. Miller, M.A. Cohen, and B. Wiersema, *Victim costs and consequences: A new look,* (NCJ 155282, U.S. Department of Justice, Office of Justice Programs, National Institute of Justice, 1996), https://www.ncjrs.gov/pdffiles/victcost.pdf.

12. D. Finkelhor, G. Hotaling, I.A. Lewis, and C. Smith, *Sexual abuse in a national survey of adult men and women: Prevalence, characteristics and risk factors.* (Family Research Laboratory, University of New Hampshire, Durham 03824, 1990).

13. Richard J. Estes and Neil Alan Weiner, *Commercial Sexual Exploitation of Children in the United States, 1997–2000* (Ann Arbor, MI: Inter-university Consortium for Political and Social Research [distributor], 2006), http://www.preventtogether.org/Resources/Documents/NationalPlan2012FINAL.pdf.

14. Richard J. Estes and Neil Alan Weiner, *Commercial Sexual Exploitation of Children in the United States, 1997–2000* (Ann Arbor, MI: Inter-university Consortium for Political and Social Research [distributor], 2006), http://www.preventtogether.org/Resources/Documents/NationalPlan2012FINAL.pdf.

15. Definition of Threshold, *Merriam Webster Dictionary*, https://www.merriam-webster.com/dictionary/threshold, accessed August 15, 2017.

16. Josh. 24:15.

17. Prov. 31:28.

18. *The Fatherless Generation*, accessed October 3, 2017. https://thefatherlessgeneration.wordpress.com/statistics/.

19. John 6:51.

20. John 4:14.

21. Ps. 24:7.

Letter #3

22. T.D. Jakes, *The Lady, Her Lover, and Her Lord* (New York: Berkley Books, 1998), 92.

23. Gal. 5:1; Heb. 12:1.

24. Gen. 3:6–7.

25. James 1:15.

26. Gen. 4:7.

27. John 14:6.

28. Phil. 3:14.

Letter #4

29. Matt. 6:33.

30. Ps. 37:4.

31. Jer. 29:11.

32. Dr. Myles Munroe, *Understanding the Purpose and Power of Woman* (Pennsylvania: Whitaker House, 2001), 45–47.

33. Ps. 32:3.

34. Deut. 8:18.

35. Acts 2.

36. Rom. 8:8.

37. Rom. 8:17.

Letter #6

38. 1 Sam. 20:1.

39. 1 Sam 20:2.

40. 1 Sam 20: 41–42.

41. Eric and Leslie Ludy, *When God Writes Your Love Story* (Oregon: Loyal Publishing, 2003), 60.

Letter #7

42. Eph. 5:22.

43. Eph. 5:23.

44. 1 Pet. 5:7.

45. Esther 4:12–14.

46. Heb. 11:1.

47. Ruth 2:3.

48. Prov. 18:22.

49. Ruth 2:6–7.

50. Ruth 2:13.

Letter #8

51. Eph. 5:22–23.

52. Dr. Myles Munroe, *Understanding the Purpose and Power of Woman* (Pennsylvania: Whitaker House, 2001), 109–110.

53. Prov. 31:10–31.

54. Prov. 19:14.

55. Lynette Lewis, Mother's Day Sermon, King's Park International Church, May 10, 2015.

Journal

Journal

Journal

Journal

Journal

Journal

Journal

Journal

Journal

Journal